Seek After

On Seven Modern Lyric Poets

Seek After

On Seven Modern Lyric Poets

EDITED BY
DAVID BAKER

STEPHEN F. AUSTIN STATE UNIVERSITY PRESS
NACOGDOCHES, TEXAS

First Edition
Printed in South Korea

For information about special discounts for bulk purchases, contact *Distribution* at sfapress@sfasu.edu or 1-936-468-1078

Production Manager: Kimberly Verhines

Cover Art: "Introduction to the World" by Ellen Sheffield.

ISBN 978-1-62288-188-8

Stephen F. Austin State University Press
P.O. Box 13007 SFA Station
Nacogdoches, Texas 75962
sfapress@sfasu.edu
www.sfasu.edu/sfapress
936-468-1078

A Note on the Text

We refer to the following editions of the seven primary poets discussed in *Seek After:*

John Keats, *John Keats: A Critical Edition of the Major Works,* ed. Elizabeth Cook (Oxford University Press, 1990).

Walt Whitman, *Leaves of Grass and Other Writings,* ed. Michael Moon (W. W. Norton & Co., 2002).

Emily Dickinson, *The Complete Poems of Emily Dickinson*, ed. Thomas H. Johnson (Little, Brown and Company, 1976); *The Poems of Emily Dickinson,* ed. R. W. Franklin (Harvard University Press, 1999).

Wallace Stevens, *The Collected Poems of Wallace Stevens* (Vintage Books, 1990).

Marianne Moore, *The Poems of Marianne Moore,* ed. Grace Schulman (Viking Penguin, 2003).

Gwendolyn Brooks, *Riot* (Broadside Press, 1969).

W. S. Merwin, *The First Four Books of Poems* (Copper Canyon Press, 2000); *The Second Four Books of Poems* (Copper Canyon Press, 1992); *The Shadow of Sirius* (Copper Canyon Press, 2009); *The Vixen* (Alfred A. Knopf, 1997).

JOHN KEATS — DAVID BAKER

WALT WHITMAN — LINDA GREGERSON

EMILY DICKINSON — MEGHAN O'ROURKE

WALLACE STEVENS — CARL PHILLIPS

MARIANNE MOORE — STANLEY PLUMLY

GWENDOLYN BROOKS — ANN TOWNSEND

W. S. MERWIN — ROSANNA WARREN

Acknowledgments

Portions of this book first appeared in earlier versions in the following journals, to whose editors we extend our collective gratitude: *The Kenyon Review*, *Literary Imagination*, *The New England Review*, *Poetry*, *The Virginia Quarterly Review*, *The Writer's Chronicle*. Three of David Baker's essays were reprinted in *Show Me Your Environment: Essays on Poetry, Poets, and Poems* (University of Michigan Press).

The editor is grateful to Denison University for its support of this project. Likewise, the group of us appreciates the Associated Writing Programs for the opportunity to present these chapters as symposia and to find eager reception and feedback from the members of AWP.

Table of Contents

I long and seek after

—Sappho

The question itself has not changed
but only the depths of memory
through which it rises . . .

—W. S. Merwin

Preface

I long and seek after—. Sappho's clause aches and beckons. It is all that remains of a poem we know as her fragment #36. Perhaps, in this eroded form, it exerts even more reaching power than the original poem did. We will never know, as we will never know the original context or narrative. They are lost. In this form, we must imagine and even provide the objects that the poet's predicates and preposition point toward. Yet is its incompleteness part of the reason why Sappho's work feels so powerfully personal, so modern to us? Or, are those features—intimacy, modernity—embedded in her idiom? They feel so, especially if we compare her works to her Greek contemporaries' poems, the palinodes of Stesichorus with their epic formalism, for instance, or the odes of Pindar with their heightened, public rhetoric.

What gives a lyric poem its intimacy? What makes a lyric poem modern? These are two of the present book's sustained interrogations. In fact, I take this book's title from Sappho to point to a similar yearning that every reader of poetry must feel. We turn to a poem because we have a need, like a physical thirst. That need may be for solace after pain or loss, for courage facing doubt, for justice or empathy amid strife, or for the ordering that language can provide to chaotic feelings and events. Sometimes, perhaps, it's the simple desire to sing or be serenaded. Poetry gives us the linguistic depth not just to understand our lives, but to shape them and live them.

That is, we turn to poetry for a vision of how to live. That must have been central to Ralph Waldo Emerson's similar seeking and longing in his vision of a new country. In his great essay, "The Poet," first published in 1844—a full sixty-eight years after the Declaration of Independence was drafted—Emereson lamented that he had not yet identified any American poet whose progressive vision could match and represent the character of the nascent American democracy: "We do not, with sufficient plainness, or sufficient profoundness, address ourselves to life, nor dare we chaunt our on times and social circumstance." Emerson sought after such a "genius" who would be both aesthetically and politically representative, who would provide a new art and idiom for a new culture. And yet, he added, "I look in vain for the poet whom I describe."

More than two-and-a-half millennia after Sappho sang her poem, and 174 years after "The Poet," the seven poet-critics gathered here seek something, too. It falls to each age, each generation, each community, and each solitary reader to engage the poets of the past and reengage and realign the received judgments about their work. Sometimes our findings may confirm those articulations of sustaining value; yet often here we forge significant new ways of reading these major poets. Reputation and relevance require diligent, ongoing negotiation. It's also essential to examine ways our great modern poets change with contemporary questions and contexts. Here we look at Walt Whitman's poetry alongside the war in Iraq, for instance, and Gwendolyn Brooks and the race riots of 2011 and 2014.

Seek After is a collective study of seven of the most influential American and English poets of the last two hundred years, designed to ask these questions about modernity and the nature of the modern lyric and to both reexamine and challenge our given opinions. These seven poets—John Keats, Walt Whitman, Emily Dickinson, Wallace Stevens, Marianne Moore, Gwendolyn Brooks, and W. S. Merwin—represent for us the early, high, and recent stages of modern lyric poetry. Beyond the basic questions I've indicated, we consider how the modern develops and evolves, what its features are, how these poets represent, further shape and create, the modern lyric "tradition."

We begin with John Keats, whose short life ended nearly 200 years ago. Of course, Keats is a Romantic poet—perhaps unequaled in stature—and of course he retains, especially in his earlier work, significant vestiges of the Age of Reason and the late 18th century. But as he shifts into his late major works, primarily his odes, transferring his deepest inheritance from Milton to Shakespeare, Keats creates and anticipates some central modern precepts. Perhaps

Shakespeare "invented" the modern in literature, as Harold Bloom persuasively argues, but Keats deepens it. His radical interiority, his self-searching, his dramatic narrative of "negative capability," his aesthetic values all take him far from his epic, classical origins into the lyric of the "early modern." We might have selected Wordsworth for this position, especially for his devotion to the vernacular, to the rhetoric of speech instead of heightened song; but Keats seems even more expansive in his anticipation of the modern.

Like Keats, Walt Whitman does as much to invent the modern as he does to shape the Romantic. Whitman is the poet of New York, no doubt, spending time in significant residence in Brooklyn, Long Island, and Manhattan. From his New York experience, he becomes, in important ways, the first truly urban poet—that is, the first not merely to describe but accept and even embrace the future's metropolitan features. But few readers and scholars account sufficiently for the full decade Whitman spent in Washington D.C, from 1862-73. Thus, our focus in this chapter is on those profound years: the Civil War and after, Whitman's immersive nursing and medical experience, his flair for political hobnobbing (which he carried over from New York), and the transforming effect of the War and the wounded soldiers on his subsequent poetry. How does this great erotic poet becomes a great elegist, and how might this transformation play a part in his preparations for the modern?

If Whitman is urban and public, Emily Dickinson is equally secluded and intimate. Does she embody the first great lyric poetry of the English language written by a woman? What is the relationship of her close-held privacy and her at-times gregarious, "wild" society of poetic engagements? Here each of our four critics investigates a specific conceit of Dickinson's residential habits: her cultivations, both horticultural and aesthetic; her fastidious documentation of the domestic population, avian and human; her method of metaphor-making, like passing through a door or room or floor of a house; and ultimately her transportive sense of time and eternity. This chapter engages especially in recent critical approaches to material culture and historicism. A poem is part of a poet's wider social and cultural identity, even—or in Dickinson's case especially—when that social engagement is so fastidiously guarded and conscribed. This becomes a central feature of modern poetry, as well as the relation of cultural engagement to deepening interiority.

Wallace Stevens marks our transition to the early 20th century and "high" modernism. Other essential modernists might include Gertrude Stein, T. S. Eliot, W. B. Yeats, or Robert Frost, of course; but Stevens provides a particularly focused example of modern lyric poetry's manner of thinking, its heady sustained "esthetique." In fact, Stevens's training in and crucial usage of philosophical methods and tropes makes him the supreme exemplar of lyric speculation and academic or scholarly constructions in modernist poetics. This is his preferred society, the society of ideas. So we ask, how does the modern lyric think, and how does that intellectual depth become a manner of feeling? More bluntly, how is thinking not just a cognitive or speculative scheme for Stevens but a manner of expressive enablement: a kind of emotion? And further, what are the specific tactics of his thinking-as-emotion, the craft and style as well as the philosophical underpinning of his massive achievement?

Marianne Moore provides a second example of a high modernist lyric poet. Like Stevens, like many modernists, she deploys an expansive intellectual methodology to her project; she writes like a thinker. But for all the strategy and seriousness of her work, she is as notable for her buoyancy, her joy in observing and making. That is, if at first her poems seem nearly clinical in their proposed objectivity, her precision, her invested curiosity, and her intricate patience all suggest her manner of close-up joy more than any real objective distance. The appearance of impersonality—the deflective habit of her "self"—is in fact a primary feature of her character, her unmistakable personality. She makes art from such paradox. In Moore's work, the microscopic can become representative, if not quite universal, and her image-driven textures and surfaces can yield as much heady resonance, as much thematic depth, as in Stevens's work.

Our chapter on Gwendolyn Brooks is this book's only instance of our consideration of a single work. Brooks's poem and short book, entitled *Riot,* is a three-part masterpiece of American poetry from the late 1960s and provides our three commentators a chance to focus—one section per critic—on this long-out-of-print but essential triptych. We argue that with this work Brooks transitions from modern to postmodern aesthetics, as she remembers the Harlem Renaissance and turns to embrace, and help shape, the new Black Arts Movement. Here her work becomes more explicit in its powers of resistance, its narratives of class conflict and racial representation. This daring poem is as difficult as anything in Eliot, as multifaceted as a cubist painting, and yet by turns as direct and politically acute as anything by Muriel Rukeyser, Amiri Baraka, or Adrienne Rich. She expresses a new postmodern sensibility toward experimentation in form and voice while retaining her expansive prosodic finesse.

W. S. Merwin is the only one of the seven poets discussed in *Seek After* who is still living. Like Brooks, Merwin provides a representative bridge from late modern to postmodern poetics; and, of course, his continuation up to and beyond the millennium brings both historical currency and aesthetic transformation into our present contemporary lyric practice. From the early 1950s to the present, his work pioneers a reverse development, a purposeful unwinding of scholarly decorum: from academic formalism into the deep image and primitivist schools to the ecological imperatives of our day. It's a resolute forgetting, an erasure of learned mannerisms—the confessional voice, an intricate formal traditionalism, a poetic too readily exempt from political engagement—into a plain style that verges on "naked" archetypal expressiveness capable of powerful cultural critique as well as profound beauty. His contributions extend to include his sustained warnings as we enter the anthropocene era and his unparalleled commitment to translation of poetries from around the world.

Seek After has evolved out of a series of lectures conducted over the past decade for the Associated Writing Programs. This book purposely retains some of the informal and personal nature of the lecture format; we think this is appropriate for general readers as well as for literary scholars—for poets, teachers, students, and critics. Some readers might find that this book serves as a valuable partner to *Radiant Lyre: Essays on Lyric Poetry*, which I edited with Ann Townsend in 2007. Both books aspire to be unhobbled by academic jargon, yet deepened by the scholarly background and personal investment of each of the essayists. In fact, it has been important that each commentator is himself or herself a poet as well as a widely practiced critic and teacher, adding rich specialties to the shared project.

This editor and our panel of poet-critics wish to thank the Associated Writing Programs for the opportunity to present early versions of each chapter as symposiums at the annual AWP conventions. We are grateful to the real and virtual communities of readers and correspondents we have gathered as we have developed these essays. The editor further extends his deep thanks to Kimberly Verhines, Mark Sanders, and their colleagues at Stephen F. Austin State University Press. I am grateful for your care and support, and I am pleased at this chance to present our book to readers who may be seeking after something only a poet can give them.

John Keats

A MORTAL WITNESS

The Odes for Their Own Sake

Stanley Plumly

Between the end of April and the beginning of June 1819, John Keats wrote the spring odes that ultimately made his name and fame. They include, in the common order, "Ode to Psyche," "Ode to a Nightingale," "Ode on a Grecian Urn," "Ode on Melancholy," and "Ode on Indolence." Then, in September, on Sunday, the 19th, in the college town of Winchester, he added "To Autumn," perhaps the purest poem in the language. The compositional order of the spring odes varies according to the authority. Helen Vendler proposes one order, John Bernard another, Jackson Bate another, Susan Wolfson another, and so on. The order of the odes is well off the point of my concern here. The nature of their individual and collective importance is.

That the odes represent the future rather than the past of English-speaking poetry is, I believe, beyond question. And that they advance the groundbreaking work of Wordsworth's "Tintern Abbey" and Coleridge's conversation poems is also, I believe, certain. The odes elevate the discussion of poetry to questions of aesthetic absolutes and content transparencies. They do these things in so many multiple and simultaneous ways that they continue to engage our attention as if they had just been written—indeed, their lack of investment in history or society has been, on occasion, a source of complaint. Though not exactly art for its own sake, they do, in each instance, foreground the act of their making as well as the resolution of what has been made. No wonder Wallace Stevens honors Keats above all other precursors.

Even the critical language employed to service the odes sounds "modern," if not postmodern. Critics speak of their internal and symbolic debate; their auditory imagination; their language of paradox; their rhetoric of irony; their poetics of indeterminacy; their in-feeling of a moment; their structural polyphony. The critics then take on the odes' play with vowel sounds contemportized of mythic and biblical allusion; their amalgamation of the English and Italian sonnet forms with the Spenserian stanza into a ten-line masterpiece that begins rather secretly in the irregular "Ode to Psyche" and ends in the transformed eleven-line stanza of "To Autumn." And then the critics do their homework and create the Keatsian odal appendices, notes, commentaries, and so on. Homework that starts in the Victorian era, in 1848, that year being the first year the odes were even critically seen as possibly great poetry and possibly linked as a group—in Monckton Milne's first "biography" of Keats, a haphazard of available letters, personal memoir, and some of the poems, many published for the first time.

The odes very likely are the first sustained symbolist poetry, certainly in their influence on Poe, Dickinson, and the French. I am less interested, however, in the odes' general modernism than in their unique contribution to what becomes the chief affect of the modern poem: its relation of subject to object; of indeed the disappearance of subject into object. And one way to see the presentation of the process of this disappearance is to think of the odes in ekphrastic terms—not simply as examples of ekphrasis itself (which would, in the first place, be a stretch), but as models of how the imagined object becomes the art object and from there becomes the poem as object. This, I believe, is the aesthetic reality Keats realizes in the odes—perhaps somewhat awkwardly in "Ode to Psyche" and perhaps somewhat inadequately in "Ode on Indolence," but in the in-between odes surpassing what had been thought was possible in a lyric poem.

When I say imagined object, I mean projected object; I mean object of the heart's affection and the mind's eye. All of the "objects" Keats presents in the odes are created out of clues and collectives of information, suggestions and combinations, offerings and suppositions. His figure of Psyche comes from Lempriere's *Classical Dictionary*, *The Golden Ass* by Apuleius, and Mary Tighe's Spenserian romance entitled *Psyche*. And there is a sculpture by Canova called *Cupid and Psyche*. But these sources are groundwork to Keats's building of "a fane / In some untrodden region of my mind." They are shadows of the substance he makes of them, of their "pinions" embracing and intertwined. They underwrite his construct of his dream sculpture, his poem art. "I see, and sing, by my own eyes inspired."

"Ode on Melancholy" also addresses a goddess incorporated in front of us in a process of building, a sculpting of a "Veil'd Melancholy" who greatly resembles the hidden face of Moneta in "The Fall of Hyperion." In this case, Keats transforms the "blue devils" of a mood and feeling into the richest potential of the moment—into the guise and trophy reality of a mother-lover figure in "her sovran shrine." Besides his own emotional equipment, Keats's main source, of course, is Burton's *Anatomy of Melancholy*, a text Keats took very much to heart. The now famous cancelled first stanza of the poem points further to the fact that art and not allegory was foremost on Keats's mind. It reads:

> Though you should build a bark of dead men's bones,
>   And rear a phantom gibbet for a mast,
> Stitch creeds together for a sail, with groans
>   To fill it out, bloodstained and aghast;
> Although your rudder be a Dragon's tail,
>   Long sever'd, yet still hard with agony,
> Your cordage large uprootings from the skull
>   Of bald Medusa; certes you would fail
> To find the Melancholy, whether she
>   Dreameth in any Isle of Lethe dull.

"Ode on a Grecian Urn" is probably the most obvious example of the ekphrastic impulse. It turns in the air before us as if on an invisible potter's wheel—or else we walk around it as if it were a museum piece. And it talks as well as showing forth the frieze of its implied story. But, of course, there is no actual single funereal work in fact that Keats is looking at: the Grecian Urn is drawn from a composite of sources—though "drawn" is not the right choice, since the urn is ushered into Keats's presence *a priori*: it is already there at the outset. Keats's own "drawing," if you will, of the Sosibios vase is certainly a starting place. But there are other vases, too, such as the Borghese collection. And there is the great source Benjamin Haydon introduced Keats to at the new British Museum: the profound South Frieze of the Elgin Marbles in which a heifer is being led to sacrifice. The three figures on the urn in the "Ode on Indolence" reiterate the turning and ghosting of life perfected in the afterlife of art, where ripe fruit never falls. The urn, we might say, is death sculpture, word-picture.

The urn ode—no surprise—was first published in *The Annals of the Fine Arts* in January of 1820. The visual and plastic arts were its focus. "Ode to a Nightingale" was published in the same magazine in July of the year before. "Nightingale," therefore, is no less about a work of art than it is a work of art, a romance with a myth going back to Ovid and carried forward by any number of poets, sometimes emphasizing the Philomela tale, sometimes emphasizing the thrush's ornithology. Exquisite pain is part of it; the piercing thorn at the breast another part. The nightingale's song, that "Singest of summer in full-throated ease," is beautiful and painful at once, a correlative for the heartache of the speaker and the dream-state he finds himself in in his garden setting with dusk and dark coming on. This great ode recapitulates a whole history of the lament as music, nature as human longing, the imagination as listening. The tableau is of a piece, almost impossible to see but profound to hear. Hearing is the medium of the painting rendered *here* in auditory visual terms over a duration that complicates the moment into a sense of the sublime and a feeling of suspension, otherwise tragic in its emotion. The moment is held, the speaker and the nightingale both still, but the birdsong, like the falling dusk, moves in time, until the moment is released, the speaker lost, and the music fled.

Keats may have thought his romance with the ode was complete once the spring was over. Change of venue, though, can sometimes make all the difference. By September of 1819, he is living in Winchester, once again, for all intents and purposes, homeless. The feeling of belonging, of the need to belong, that feeling of orphaning ending permeates "To Autumn." It is a poem of homecoming. The writerly sources of the poem include a bit of Wordsworth and

Coleridge, but primarily Thomas Chatterton and his autumnal "Aella." The cornucopia myth surrounding the corn goddess Ceres also figures in. Mostly, however, this is a poem prefigured by pastoral pictorial traditions, including Claude, Gainsborough, Poussin, Romano, and William Hamilton. It is the pastoral word-picture of all word-pictures. Keats drafted it on a Sunday in Winchester, anticipating autumn, its "fine air," its "temperate sharpness," its "chaste weather." It is largely based on his daily walks between the college grounds along the River Itchen and its water meadows and the hospice at St. John's—a distance of about a mile and a half, one way. "I never lik'd stubble fields so much as now," he writes in a letter to his friend John Reynolds. "Somehow a stubble plain looks warm—in the same way that some pictures look warm—this struck me so much in my sunday's walk that I composed upon it." He composes on it by extending, ever so much, the vital form of the spring odes by one line per stanza, just enough to enlarge the space and enrich the depth of field.

Can a lyric poem of thirty-three lines achieve the awe and spaciousness of the sublime? "To Autumn" is a tone poem for sure, a twilit symbolist masterpiece realized independently—it seems—of its implied author, as if it were an object, self-created, within the harvest terms of itself. Further, the subtlety of the poem's inherent voice make it seem that as a maker, Keats has disappeared into the text, absorbed by it in the act of seeing it—seeing, interpreting, transforming the landscape now so familiar to him on his almost daily walks. It is also a painting in the sense that its visual, imagistic information is theatrically blocked out so as to be simultaneous yet sequential as the eye moves from foreground to middle ground to background—from "thatch eves" and "cottage trees" to "granary floor" and "brook" to "barred clouds" and "stubble plains" and "gathering swallows . . . in the skies." It is this specific Sunday's view of a last-summer-day's-beginning-of-autumn-day's transition, season to season, and at once this vision of eternal autumn, its mists, its fullness, its gatherings, its drowsiness, and its warmths that sets it apart. It is the full cup emptied, filled then unfilled. The tone, therefore, is residually spiritual, elevated beyond the "autumnal" emotion; the feeling is one of surpassing exhaustion—"ripeness to the core," "o'er-brimmed," "last oozings hours by hours"—the pluralizing of our responses; the vision, ultimately, is of "the soft-dying day," the wind living then dying, "the wailful choir" of it all—vegetable, animal, human—singing while listening. Each of the great Keatsian odes suspends in lyric tragedy—none more purely and resonantly than "To Autumn," whose visionary size transcends its local space.

"To Autumn," then, is a painting, a transparency of language made of language as an object in itself, as paint and plaster and stone are. Word-painting, word-sculpture, poem-art—whatever characterization you choose—the odes are art objects whose identities are defined by the content of the materials they are made of. They are original insofar as they are imagined, made of and from their various disparate sources, expressed in terms appropriate to their individual natures. The hand of their maker disappears into the language of the making, so that the song of the nightingale is visible as well as audible as an ode, the attic shape of the urn is three-dimensional as it turns within the space of its ode, the declension toward and above the autumn horizon line of the harvest advances in narrative sequence as meaningful as it is beautiful. The rhetoric here is representational, the plastic of the poem a thing apart.

Corresponding Keats

DAVID BAKER

John Keats lived a very short life. He was born on Halloween at a livery stable north of London, in 1795, and died in a little room at 26 Piazza di Spagna in Rome, on February 23, 1821. "[W]ith the most perfect ease—he seemed to go to sleep," as Joseph Severn wrote in a short shattering letter to Charles Brown a few days later. John Keats's window of opportunity for writing poetry was as narrow as a castle arrow-slit—even more so when we recall that he wrote his six great odes in just a few months: one in April and four in May of 1819, then the magnificent and ultimate "To Autumn" that September. He was so sick with tuberculosis (or consumption, as they called it, though his doctor in Italy misdiagnosed that the young poet suffered from "a stomach ailment"—what awful care he received; he should never have died then) that he didn't write poetry for the last year and several months of his life. He really wrote poetry for about five years. Think of that.

He also wrote letters. Before he wrote poems and after he had stopped writing poems and all during the relative outpouring of poems, he wrote hundreds of pages of letters. And that—or, more exactly, his habit of correspondence together with his manner of corresponding—is my double subject here. Keats's letters are fascinating and various, full and wild, forlorn, lovelorn, art-struck, heat-struck, fever-struck, feisty, argumentative, headstrong, absolutely certain, and absolutely unsure, unsteady, and undone by just about everything.

Perhaps I should reveal here that I don't read many letters. I enjoy receiving them, when I get a real one these days. But I don't often turn to those dusty volumes of letters written by literary authors. Nor do I read biographies, of anybody, except for some reason of Walt Whitman and sometimes John Clare. There is an art to the letter, however, and I know it's a stale observation to say that the art of the epistle is in danger, having been circumvented lately by the internet and email and twitter and Skype and IM and even the familiar telephone. I do have to say that the literary blog, as a vigorous entity, is serving some of the function of the literary letter these days—full of passion and opinion, encouragement and genuine criticism, as well as rant and manifesto, snark and self-serving advertisement. But I love the paper, the style and depth, the manner of talk of the real thing.

The first letter we have of Keats's—though it's unlikely the first letter he actually wrote—is from sometime in November 1815, and addressed to G. F. Mathew. George Felton Mathew, along with his two girl cousins, Caroline and Ann, was an early friend of Keats. Mathew may later have written poems about Keats; he certainly did review Keats's first book of poems, and he probably provided information later when Richard Monckton Milnes was putting together an early biography of the poet. This first letter, of all things, comes in the form of a poem in rhymed couplets, a truly epistolary poem in the manner of Pope. This was a habit of Keats's, early in his correspondence, to write letters-as-poems. They are full of adolescent Romanticism, as the opening lines of this one indicate:

> Sweet are the pleasures that to verse belong,
> And doubly sweet a brotherhood in song;
> Nor can remembrance, Mathew! bring to view
> A fate more pleasing, a delight more true
> Than that in which the brother Poets joy'd,
> Who with combined powers, their wit employ'd
> To raise a trophy to the drama's muses.
> . . . .
> Fain would I echo back each pleasant note
> As o'er Sicilian seas, clear anthems float
> 'Mong the light skimming gondolas far parted,
> Just when the sun his farewell beam has darted:
> But 'tis impossible; far different cares
> Beckon me sternly from soft "Lydian airs,"
> And hold my faculties so long in thrall,

> That I am oft in doubt whether at all
> I shall again see Phoebus in the morning:
> Or flush'd Aurora in the roseate dawning!

The classical references in this letter range from Sicilian seas, Lydia, Aurora, Phoebus, to the Druids and faeries of the Celtic past. And literary allusions to *The Fairie Queene*, Milton's "L'Allegro," Pope's "Essay on Man," and more. He even makes a specific reference to the Scotsman, William Wallace—whom we may know from Mel Gibson's caricature. His early letters are also full of personal detail, tucked inside the allusive, expansive, rather teenaged sceneries, as I'll touch on shortly.

Keats's last letter seems to have been the famous farewell note of November 30, 1820. This would be nearly three full months before his death on February 23, 1821. He is writing from his bed in the room at the foot of the Spanish Steps engaged by Dr. Clark for the two travelers Keats and Severn. Here is the opening of this incredible and fairly short letter:

> 'Tis the most difficult thing in the world for to me to write a letter. My stomach continues so bad, that I feel it worse on opening any book,—yet I am much better than I was in Quarantine. Then I am afraid to encounter the proing and conning of any thing interesting to me in England. I have an habitual feeling of my real life having past, and that I am leading a posthumous existence.

He closes this letter to his dear friend Charles Brown with heartbreaking directness—and a final sentence of prose which also scans as perfect iambic tetrameter:

> Write to George as soon as you receive this, and tell him how I am, as far as you can guess; and also a note to my sister—who walks about my imagination like a ghost—she is so like Tom. I can scarcely bid you good bye even in a letter. I always made an awkward bow.

Keats's letters are better than most poets' poems. It seems to have been one of those literary cottage industries of the mid-20th century to examine and reproduce Keats's letters. Among the most useful editions is Maurice Buxton Forman's *The Letters of John Keats*, published by Oxford in 1931. Forman provides a good introduction, and as it becomes more and more idiosyncratic among the letter-editors, he gives a set of interesting, if sometimes strange, biographical blurbs on Keats's correspondents. But he did a good early job of selecting among the letters, and this seems to have been the base text used by Lionel Trilling, in his edition *The Selected Letters of John Keats*, in 1951.

Trilling's edition is unsurprisingly clear and astute. His biographies are direct, if not downright abbreviated. It's Trilling's long introduction that I find so appealing, though sometimes a bit odd. He says: "The charm of Keats's letters is almost inexhaustible, and we can scarcely hope to define it wholly or to name all its elements." Which he then proceeds to do: He "took life in the largest possible way." He expressed a "conscious impulse to live life in the heroic mode." His life was defined by "intuition, courage, and the accumulation of experience." His mind was a "kind of magical confrontation." And this all comes from just half a page in Trilling's long introduction. Trilling seems drawn to the century-old figure of Keats as tragic martyr, so full of poetry that his feeble body couldn't contain it for long. Feeble body: I should add that diminutive John Keats was a rather ferocious boxer, before his illness, muscled and cantankerous and powerful. It's only after the contraction of consumption that he dwindled and became the stereotypical stricken Romantic poet—pale, withered, ethereal, ghostly, slight, as the familiar tropes go.

No less and no stranger than George Bernard Shaw calls Keats a genial correspondent. Lionel Trilling agrees. I'm not sure about that. These letters seem to me more intense than genial, poetry-filled and full of passion and conviction. They are typified by that familiar Romantic urgency with all things Art and Poesy and Keats's own "Beauty is truth, truth beauty." They are typified by pronouncement and arm-sweeping passion. Genial? I don't know.

But I do know we can learn more about poetry, especially of the Romantic flavor, from Keats's letters than from many other poets' actual poetic work. No less than T. S. Eliot, that famous grouch with hardly one good word for anything Romantic, claimed that Keats's letters are "certainly the most notable and the most important ever written by an English poet." I'm drawing the following illustrations from the best edition of his letters, *The Letters of John Keats 1814-1821*, edited by Hyder E. Rollins and published in 1958 at Harvard. This complete collection comes with an exhaustive chronology, a lucid introduction, and all the attending materials, including the best footnotes to the letters that we have. Only a few other scholars have offered so much real detail and knowing sympathy as Rollins; I'm referring to the likes of Walter Jackson Bate and Stanley Plumly.

Here are just a couple of passages from the Rollins edition. I think you'll find a familiar note, an essential note, in each of these. To his brothers George and Thomas, just before Christmas in 1817, he writes with a depth of understanding rare in criticism, let alone in letters: "at once it struck me, what quality went to form a Man of Achievement especially in Literature & which Shakespeare possessed so enormously—I mean *Negative Capability*, that is when man is capable of being in uncertainties, Mysteries, doubts, without any irritable reaching after fact & reason." To Richard Woodhouse, on October 27, 1818, he writes as if to anticipate the Emersonian Oversoul that "as to the poetical Character itself, (I mean that sort of which, if I am anything, I am a Member; that sort distinguished from the wordsworthian or egotistical sublime; which is a thin per se and stands alone) it is not itself—it has no self—it is every thing and nothing—It has no character—it enjoys light and shadow; it lives in gusto, be it foul or fair, high or low, rich or poor, mean or elevated." To James Hessey he writes with aphoristic brilliance, on October 8, 1818, that "The Genius of Poetry must work out its own salvation in a man. . . . That which is creative must create itself." There are so many such insightful moments and observations in his letters.

As I was reading the letters again, turning back and forth to the poems, I was struck as never before by the correspondence between those two modes of communication. It's been my thinking—my incorrect thinking, as it turns out—that Keats's poems are singular, consistently self-inturning. In fact, I see now that Keats's poems are correspondences to an astonishing degree. He was a talker, a teacher, an arguer, and he wanted not just an audience but real respondents in his readers—not just in his letters but also in his poems. So while Shaw's term about Keats's geniality isn't quite right, it is close. I'd call it something like sociability. Some of this must stem from the loneliness of the man, the paucity in his real life of a sustained literary cadre. But just consider the following list. I went once more through his complete poems. His poems are written to, in direct address to, are literally forms of correspondence to: Spenser, Byron, Lord Chatterton, Leigh Hunt, Apollo (these are the first five poems of his that we have), G. F. Mathew, one "who has been long in city pent," brother George, Charles Cowden Clark, all his brothers, Haydon, Milton, Shakespeare, a friend, a "lady seen for a few moments at Vauxhall," John H. Reynolds (my favorite of his epistolary poems is addressed to Reynolds, the poem where he coins the delicious term "the material sublime"), Homer, some "sweet maidens," Maia, the poet Burns, the "bards of passion," the "wretched wight," Fanny Brawne, and more.

But I noticed another, very eerie change in the correspondents. As the poems proceed in time, as Keats transforms from the vigorous young poet into the ailing and failing one, his epistolary audiences change as well. They turn from actual people into ideas personified, or not even personified. All along, to be sure, he might address a poem to the figure of the wind, or a grasshopper; but by the time he's dying, Keats is no longer writing poems to people at all. His companions and correspondents are more like Platonic ideals: He writes an ode to Sleep, an ode to Psyche, another to a Nightingale. Of course, to Autumn.

The rhetorical demeanor and detailing of the poems change, too. Like the letters, the earlier poems are full of oddity, associative leaps, and a rather gregarious personality, making both high and low-fallutin gestures. At the end, especially in the odes, Keats is writing with an otherworldly clarity and compression, a distilled and at least partly "posthumous" perspective. He's writing not from this life, and not to citizens of this world, but he is writing instead from the other side, after the fact, when "the day is gone, and all its sweets are gone" as he mourns in his last sonnet, when he hears the music of "the soft-dying day" of an autumnal and vanishing existence.

If his poems are letters, as I think it's useful to regard them, then the recipients of these epistles undergo a dramatic transfiguration, from the real to the ideal, from people to the more purely poetic.

Something else has always bothered me, something I couldn't for the longest time identify. Here is a telling phrase—and assertion—from another of Keats's letters. He's writing on May 3rd, 1818, to Reynolds. As he talks about his aesthetic allegiances shifting back and forth from Milton to Wordsworth, Pope to Gray, Hazlitt to Patmore, he says: "I must be quaint, and free of Tropes and figures." In this letter, to be sure, his tone is witty and playful, ironic, complex. But I hear that self-directed imperative as a real desire, too. In fact, this is a rather stunning repositioning of aesthetic practice for Keats. How is it that this poet, whose work is so densely packed with allusion, figure, troping, conceit, now hopes to be free of tropes and figures?

I want to be even more specific, for I have noticed an important modification in Keats's work—an actual shift in the nature and kind of his troping. I noted earlier the way his correspondence changes, from people to ideals. But his manner of making correspondences also changes—the way he compares, the way he tropes.

Here is a short verse paragraph from the Reynolds epistle:

> The doors all look as if they oped themselves,
> The windows as if latched by fays and elves,
> And from them comes a silver flash of light,
> As from the westward of a summer's night;
> Or like a beauteous woman's large blue eyes
> Gone mad thro' olden songs and poesies.

We have here, in just six lines, four very central similes or comparative conditionals starting with "like" or "as." So I acted on a hunch. I counted the six odes. "Ode to Psyche" with its sixty-seven lines. "Ode to a Nightingale," the longest, at eighty. "Ode on a Grecian Urn" has fifty, while "Ode on Melancholy," the shortest, holds thirty. "Ode on Indolence" has sixty lines, and "To Autumn," the only ode not self-identified as an ode, has thirty-three. The great six odes run to three hundred and twenty lines. And in them all, all together, Keats employs three similes. Three. There were more in the little fragment I just quoted.

I should also add that these three odic similes are of minor figuration, almost accidental, certainly incidental. In the nightingale ode, he says, near the end, the word "forlorn" is "like a bell." Then he moves on. In the indolence ode, he self-references the Grecian ode, describing three figures who "pass'd, like figures on a marble urn." And in the middle of the autumn ode, he says that autumn is "sometimes like a gleaner." These are undeveloped images in the middle of intricately metaphorical poems.

What's underlies Keats's change? Is the change significant? We do tend to regard metaphor and simile as closely related figures of speech.

So here is an abbreviated version. A metaphor is a figure of speech where one thing, or its attributes, is compared directly to another thing; in fact, it becomes that other thing. It is—and here I'm blending the Princeton and Longman encyclopedia definitions—a figurative expression of similarity or dissimilarity by direct and non-literal substitution. The sun is a silver dollar.

Our standard definition of simile holds that simile is a specific kind of metaphor, a subset of the trope; it is a metaphoric linkage by means of "like" or "as." The Longman calls it a rhetorical and poetical figure of speech where particular attributes of a thing are explicitly compared to another using the words "like," "as," or "as if." That is, *the sun is* like *a silver dollar*. Or *the sun* shines like *a silver dollar*. Simile is a kind of metaphor, just a bit less direct, with a mediating and self-conscious linguistic linkage.

Keats turns away from simile, and toward metaphor, as he turned toward the odes, just as his epistolary audience turned from people into abstractions, and as his poems increased dramatically in intensity and hurried purpose. In fact, in a fascinating letter to Benjamin Haydon, written on January 23rd, 1818, Keats anticipates or prefigures the change in his poetic demeanor when he surmises that the nature of his own new poem, "Hyperion," "will lead me to . . . a more naked and grecian Manner." He doesn't finish "Hyperion," of course, but this future-tense estimation speaks directly to the clarified intensity of the odes.

I find this difference notable and significant. He wants direct and unfigured and exact correspondence; he wants transfiguration, not likeness, just as these poems seek the ultimate, even platonic source. The difference between simile and metaphor is, first of all, the difference between the transference of likeness and actual substitution; between similarity and cognitive transfiguration. Intellectual observation or judgment versus, well, something like magic.

But I'm going to turn a bit more theoretical here. I want to claim that simile holds the potential for difference in a way that metaphor makes its claim for sameness. Simile, in my thinking, argues in fact for the thing as *opposite* the other thing, in opposition to, in difference from; it enacts that kind of agon. So if, in metaphor, the sun is a silver dollar, and in simile the sun is *like* a silver dollar, then simile also reminds us that the sun is *not* a silver dollar, only in a partial way *like* one. The difference remains and is, in fact, made explicit and fixed. The sun may have an attribute of that coin (its silverness, perhaps, or its shine) but it retains its separate characterizing identity as sun.

My final point about these tropes, and Keats's early and late poetry, is drawn from this notion of sameness and difference, from likeness and transformation. I want to propose that simile tends to be ironic, requiring a doubling of the cognitive process. The thing both is and is not like the other thing. Simile is a feature of social wit—a favorite trope, not surprisingly, of poets like Pope and Swift and Byron, whom the younger Keats favored—doubled in its playful, winking knowledge. It's a manner of socially agreed-on irony, saying a thing but acknowledging its concurrent opposite. It resists completion of the transfer. Metaphor, at least in Keats's treatment, tends to be singular, obsessed, and possessed of a kind of radical sincerity and accomplishment. Again, likeness (and unlikeness) versus transformation.

So finally—as I quickly assess the distance traveled—these closing lines from Keats's second poem, "To Lord Byron," written in 1814, show the young poet's work to be generic in its romanticism and descriptive of life yet-unlived, where even "woe" can be artfully "pleasing." In this epistolary sonnet Keats addresses Byron as a swan in lines figured with simile:

> thou thy griefs dost dress
> With a bright halo, shining beamily,
> *As when* a cloud the golden moon doth veil,
> Its sides are tinged with a resplendent glow,
> Through the dark robe oft amber rays prevail,
> And *like* fair veins in sable marble flow;
> Still warble, dying swan! still tell the tale,
> The enchanting tale, the tale of pleasing woe.

Two years later, writing a sonnet letter to George, he can still barely imagine "what, without the social thought of thee, would be the wonders of the sky and sea?"

The social thought indeed. Yet in three more years, in the great odes, the question may be muted but it is also now answered. Addressing the nightingale, Keats's melancholy voice has a power, a clarity, and an astonishing purity of metaphor and syntax. Indeed, what is there, beyond the social order of the world? He sees it:

> The weariness, the fever, and the fret
> Here, where men sit and hear each other groan;
> Where palsy shakes a few, sad, last gray hairs,
> Where youth grows pale, and spectre-thin, and dies;
> Where but to think is to be full of sorrow
> And leaden-eyed despairs,
> Where Beauty cannot keep her lustrous eyes,
> Or new Love pine at them beyond to-morrow.

Myopic Keats

Ann Townsend

At fifteen, John Keats was apprenticed to an Edmonton surgeon, thus setting in motion a series of events that would fundamentally alter his poetic vision. After six years of medical training, first in Edmonton and later at Guy's Hospital in London, Keats recognized that he was too much of a dreamer to be a surgeon. Though he evidently acquitted himself well during his training, his mind was elsewhere. Troubled, he told his friend Charles Armitage Brown, "My last operation was the opening of a man's temporal artery. I did it with the utmost nicety, but reflecting on what passed through my mind at the time, my dexterity seemed a miracle, and I never took up the lancet again." He made an early choice to forsake one calling, the practice of medicine, in favor of another, the practice of poetry. But medicine, its material facts, its vocabulary, and its sense of mortal consequence, left its mark. When Keats came of age as a poet, he carried that language with him; it enlarged and enhanced the imaginative sympathy which he came to call "negative capability."

How did working knowledge of the body help him forge his own visionary imagination? First, vision suggests perspective, a critical and linguistic lens. Keats spent the ages of fifteen to twenty-one as a student of the body, and this knowledge infuses his work and informs his poetic images. Second, Keats experienced the visual world with faulty equipment: His eyes were bad. He was myopic, severely nearsighted. He saw through the mediating lenses of his spectacles. Without them, his eyes functioned only to see objects in close proximity. Third, seeing and perceptive (or intellectual) comprehension go hand-in-hand for Keats. If, in conversation, I explain something to you, then ask, "Do you see?" and you answer, "Yes, I see," what you mean is, "Yes, I understand." Keats's own vision of his place among the poets was shaped by his consciousness of the physical frailties he suffered during his few productive years as a writer. That vision was revised most profoundly on the evening when he first coughed blood and understood that he would die of the same tuberculosis that took his mother, his uncle, and his brother Tom. Each of these altered states of vision affects the pattern of Keats's artistry. No one, after a certain age, sees with entirely innocent eyes.

To be a visionary in the Romantic sense is to seek the beautiful and the divine as it resides in the human spirit itself. To be a visionary is to acknowledge the infinite possibilities inside an individual mind and spirit. Following after and reacting against the super-rationalist 18th century, the Romantic poets re-legitimized and foregrounded their emotional interior lives, valued the irrational and the imaginative, embraced the natural world, and put their faith in the evidence of the senses and what Keats called "the holiness of the Heart's affections." Keats's visionary sensibilities, however, differ from the flights and heights of Shelley or Wordsworth. His formal imaginings draw on more material and direct experience, and on a sensibility shaped by the knowledge of his own mortality.

For an analysis of artists affected by their own bodily limitations, it's worth reading Patrick Trevor-Roper's eccentric and rather delightful book, *The World through Blunted Sight*. Trevor-Roper, an ophthalmologist by training, argues that deficiencies in sight (like near and far-sightedness, color-blindness, and other diseases of the eye) inevitably influence how an artist or writer experiences and therefore depicts the world. Trevor-Roper speculates that myopes like Keats tend to gravitate toward activities that reward close attention, introspection, even isolation. He believes that an artist's near-sightedness produces an introspective sensibility, and that this sensibility affects the work itself. In practical terms, for instance, if a near-sighted person cannot take in long vistas, he or she will instead seek objects of attention, or subject matter, close at hand.

So he argues that it was natural for Percy Bysshe Shelley, who was far-sighted, to create poems that themselves capture a wide scope, with their far-off vistas, mountain ranges, and expansive landscapes. Near-sighted Keats, on the other hand, favored images that are self-limiting, close-up, and auditory rather than visual. The sense of hearing, Trevor-Roper suggests, is intensified in Keats's work for neurological reasons: When the sense of sight is damaged or limited, the other senses develop greater sensitivity in order to compensate for the loss.

"Ode to a Nightingale" is dominated by strategies of sound, by blindness, mist, and darkness. The nightingale is invisible, unseen, "light-winged dryad of the trees / In some melodious plot / Of beechen green, and shadows numberless. . . . " But its song fills the poem so completely, and Keats's capacity for imaginative hearing is so acute, that he is able to cast himself as if into the body of the birdsong. The world around him grows dark, fades far away. The poem foregrounds, wishes for, revels in, and then loses the song of the nightingale. In this poem, interior or imaginative experience is intensified because sight is absent or blunted. It's only on "the viewless wings of Poesy" that the writer may be transported. Indeed, the nightingale's song is the gift that prompts the activation of the visionary imagination.

I am charmed by the thought that the one physical trait that Keats and I apparently share—our myopia—could have helped to compel his particular poetic sensibilities. It is finally impossible to know whether Keats's myopia had a substantive effect on his poetry; to assume any further would risk reducing poetry to a clinical diagnosis. But I would argue that Keats repeatedly returns to what we call "the mind's eye"—that is, the imagination. If nearsightedness circumscribed Keats's relationship to the physical world, it makes sense that he might have developed an interest in issues of perception. He might have been inclined to turn inward rather than outward. It's right there in the final stanza of "Ode to Psyche," where his speaker seeks to

> build a fane
> In some untrodden region of my mind,
> Where branched thoughts, new grown with pleasant pain,
> Instead of pines shall murmur in the wind:
> Far, far around shall those dark-cluster`d trees

Fledge the wild-ridged mountains steep by steep;
. . . .
And in the midst of this wide quietness
A rosy sanctuary will I dress
With the wreath`d trellis of a working brain,
With buds, and bells, and stars without a name. . . .

In 1815, after leaving his initial apprenticeship with the surgeon Thomas Hammond, Keats enrolled in the medical school at Guy's Hospital in London. There he completed the studies that allowed him to take and pass his licensing exams, thus qualifying to practice as an apothecary (equivalent to our contemporary general practitioner). In the process Keats studied chemistry, anatomy, and botany, explored the intricacies of human physiology, practiced dissections, set broken bones, diagnosed diseases, and learned how to create the necessary remedies.

But after completing his education, he decided, to the dismay of his guardian, Richard Abbey, to abandon the practice of medicine in favor of the more tenuous life of poetry. He wrote, in his letter to Abbey, that he hoped to "rely upon my ability as a poet." When Abbey objected, Keats said, "my mind is made up….I know that I possess abilities greater than most men, and therefore I am determined to gain my living by exercising them." Though his guardian called him a "silly boy," these years of medical training were not wasted on Keats. When, shortly thereafter, Keats's brother Tom grew ill with the tuberculosis that eventually killed him, Keats nursed him during his final illness. And medicine also gave Keats a more intangible set of skills.

When he defines negative capability, what Keats describes is a process that sounds very much like that of the clinically objective gaze a surgeon must cultivate in order to see, to diagnose, and to heal. One must, he says, remain "open to uncertainty, mystery, and doubt …without any irritable reaching after fact and reason." So must the doctor begin by observing illness, dissection, and the workings of the body. In the same letter, Keats goes on to compare "human life to a large mansion of many apartments." He charts out only two of these apartments, the doors "to the rest being as yet shut upon me." The first is "the infant or thoughtless chamber, in which we remain as long as we do not think—we remain there a long while, and notwithstanding the doors of the second chamber remain wide open, show a bright appearance, we care not to hasten to it; but are at length imperceptibly impelled by the awakening of the thinking principle—within us...." Then: "we no sooner get into the second chamber, which I shall call the chamber of maiden-thought, than we become intoxicated with the light and the atmosphere." Just as the operating chamber, the surgical theater, is filled with lights and ether, so is the mind's chamber endowed with both mystery and a sense of mortality. In the final stanza of "Ode to Psyche," when Keats turns inward to make a home for Psyche in his mind's safe harbor, he creates a landscape that replicates what was then known about the structures of the brain, down to its divided spaces, and its ridges, branches, and trellises. Imagination and artistic creation reside, in this poem, inside the sheltering, nurturing landscape of the mind.

Keats's years of medical training gave him the materials to construct that "fane / In some untrodden region of my mind," a healing space for sleep, and quiet breathing. But, of course, he was not able to heal himself. On February 3, 1820, Keats recognized that he was about to enter the country of "embalmed darkness" when he diagnosed his own tuberculosis. That evening he had coughed blood into his pillow. He knew it was arterial blood, a sign that his lungs were fatally compromised. "Bring me the candle," he called to his friend Charles Armitage Brown, "let me see this blood." "He looked up in my face," Brown wrote, "with a calmness of countenance that I can never forget, and said, 'I know the colour of that blood; it is arterial blood. I cannot be deceived in that colour. That drop of blood is my death-warrant; I must die.'" Brown recalls Keats's calmness in the face of this appalling self-diagnosis.

The poet's work is to serve, in Stanley Plumly's phrase, as a "mortal witness." This is a role Keats willingly takes on. In "Ode to a Nightingale," Keats negotiates the essential divisions that define our human nature. The poem travels through alternating states of pain and joy, numbness and sensation, intimations of life and death. Keats uses the same word to describe both the nightingale and death; the bird sings with "full-throated ease" at the end of stanza one and, in the sixth stanza, death is "easeful." Life and death are held in abeyance, and Keats embraces neither one nor the other. The capacity for divided sight is the essence of negative capability. Keats's poems consistently put forward a poetical character that is not fixed, not formed, but always in the process of becoming. After all, as Keats writes of Apollo, god of poetry and of healing, in "Hyperion: A Romance": The poet is "a sage, / A humanist, physician to all men." The ability to remain open to uncertainty, mystery, doubt, "without any irritable reaching after fact and reason" is an asset for those who would practice either medicine or poetry.

The biographical facts that link vision to the visionary in Keats's poems cannot explain the enduring achievement, the imponderable connection between experience and art, history and achievement. Still, I think of his example when I consider my own relationship to the loved, material world. When Dr. Flood, my capable physician, peers into my eyes with her bright light and gives me the latest news of my own vision's diminishment, I am grateful that I still have time left to witness and record. Time to be a mortal witness, that is.

Walt Whitman

WAR AND THE WASHINGTON YEARS

Song of Sanity: Whitman in Washington

David Baker

He was a poet of hope and encouragement, but his greatest poem is bleak at heart, ripped bloody, and shredded with despair. He was our verbal cheerleader, our avid egoist as well as our most enthusiastic inclusionist:

> O to make the most jubilant song!
> Full of music—full of manhood, womanhood, infancy!
> Full of common employments—full of grain and trees!
>
> O for the voices of animals!

Thus he warbles, making room with his constant, necessary roll-call for us all in "A Song of Joys." Yet his greatest poem finds him desolate, solitary, at a complete loss for words, which is death for him. He was the poet of Brooklyn and Manhatta—he likes the native names for places—but his greatest poem was written in Washington, D.C., where he lived for ten years in a series of rooms and boarding houses.

I'm referring to "When Lilacs Last in the Dooryard Bloom'd." Its magnitude, its lyric intensity, the scope and rhetorical dynamics of its moving scheme, its sheer beauty as song and psalm, all become one matchless thing. But the distance it travels—literally from Washington, D.C. to Abraham Lincoln's grave in Springfield, Illinois; but more so, figuratively, from natural description to war-torn destruction and despair, to death, and beyond death back (or forward) to language and hope of a habitable world—is as massive as Virgil's epic or Dante's or Milton's, and more humane than them all. Here are the opening two sections:

1.

When lilacs last in the dooryard bloom'd,
And the great star early droop'd in the western sky in the night,
I mourn'd, and yet shall mourn with every-returning spring.

Ever-returning spring, trinity sure to me you bring,
Lilac blooming perennial and drooping star in the west,
And thought of him I love.

2.

O powerful western falling star!
O shades of night—O moody, tearful night!
O great star disappear'd—O the black murk that hides the star!
O cruel hands that hold me powerless—O helpless soul of me!
O harsh surrounding cloud that will not free my soul.

In this poem, eventually, in its most incredible scene, Whitman, the poet and our travel-guide, is dead. To "effuse" himself in eddies, to dismantle the body, to die back into nature or the natural body of others, is not in itself an unusual trope for Whitman. He plays the martyr and the victim with equal conviction as he plays the hero or abiding commoner. Yet here his death feels more existentially factual and barren than in any other of his poems. He dies in real, palpable despair. His leader, his "Captain, my Captain," has been murdered by a zealous man at the end of a vicious war. His faith in democracy and improvement has been blown apart. Nor has he, as he had prophesied, seen his beloved country "absorb him [and his poetry] as affectionately as he has absorbed it." His death is an empathic association with the dead president but also enacts the larger erasure of hope. Even the violets he sees "peep[ing] from the ground" and the "gray debris" in the old woods reflect the colors of the brutal armies.

So Whitman, or his blasted spirit, fades to the swamp, a primordial world neither solid nor fluid. And the great talker listens: to a bird, the "solitary singer" hermit thrush whose song in section fourteen is a praise-song to death, alternately identified as lovely, soothing, delicate, and cool-enfolding. Whitman's own earlier phrase is even more to my point. He says in part seven, in anticipation of the thrush and in an uncharacteristic conditional voice: "thus would I chant a song for you O sane and sacred death." The poet of life is, in his greatest poem, the poet of death.

The sacred nature of death in Whitman's poetry is clear enough. Even the names by which he refers to the lilac elegy indicate his reverent purposes. As the poem proceeds, he calls this song a dirge, a chant, a serenade, a carol, and finally—and in this order—a "powerful psalm in the night." The secular is the sacred for Whitman always. Rather it's the sane element of death that catches my eye here. How is death sane? Death is chaos otherwise and in other poetry. What does it mean to be sane?

In Whitman's first great poem, "Song of Myself," the poet commences with a vision of things. I mean that literally. Whitman is an avid watcher, a self-confessed if typically wholesome ogler. He loves to look. His imagination is initiated by sight. He "observes" a leaf of summer grass, as here in the lilac elegy he first sees a lilac bloom and the planet Venus.

The romantic trope of sight is charged with sensory immediacy. We don't have to think to observe. Or perhaps sight, with its optic nerve wired so directly into our reptile brain, is our first thinking. I look up to the sky and say "I see the sun." But notice how immediately the little clause translates to inner cognitive awareness. When we finally understand that nasty math problem, what do we say? We say, "Oh! I see!" Whitman looks and looks. He "wander[s] all night in [his] vision." "Look for me," he flirts and challenges, "under your boot-soles."

Whitman's fundamental dependence on sight complies readily and eagerly with his intellectual father, Ralph Waldo Emerson, for whom that wacky, evocative "transparent eyeball" is a central figure. Emerson watches as the light of understanding flows into and back out of the poetic mind and political body alike. Who is more felicitous, light with his touch, than Emerson? "The simple perception of natural forms is a delight," he writes. "The health of the eye seems to demand a horizon." (All along we want to respell "eye" as its homonym pronoun to enjoy Emerson's polite visionary pun.) "We are never tired, so long as we can see far enough."

Part of the appeal of sight to Emerson is its antiseptic quality. The good Unitarian Brahmin, the gentle man, didn't have to get his hands dirty if he could just look. He was dignified, a little fussy. He could be aloof. In one of the few instances we know of Emerson's loss of control, as he documents in his diary on March 29, 1832, "I visited Ellen's tomb & opened the coffin." This is the whole entry. His beloved wife had died on February 7, 1831, and her death shook Waldo to the bone. And so, even a year later, in an "act [that] remains so unnatural as to seem almost insane," according to Gay Wilson Allen, Emerson needed once more not merely to mourn his wife, but see her, visit her, take a look. Did he, as one commentator imagines, also touch her? How could he not? Did he lie down beside her?

The striking feature here is the unclean impulse of Emerson's typically antiseptic and reliably sane demeanor. A year's-dead unembalmed body in a family tomb would not be sanitary, as visiting that body would not be "sane." Touching makes us crazy.

As I said, Whitman's first impulse is visual. He's a great observer with sweeping, panoramic skills. In "Crossing Brooklyn Ferry," when he looks down into the East River, he sees his reflection in the tidal waters. But he sees also the image of the commuters passing, the ships of nations, even Manhattan's skyline. He sees the movement of generations, time itself, history, all humanity. Whitman's visual impulse is connective. But his transcendental figurations can also be blurring. He looks with such sweeping expanse that sometimes he sees only types, not particulars. Here is a scene from "First O Songs for a Prelude," one of Whitman's early Civil War poems:

Arm'd regiments arrive every day, pass through the city, and
embark from the wharves,
(How good they look as they tramp down to the river, sweaty,
with their guns on their shoulders!
How I love them! how I could hug them, with their brown
faces and their clothes and knapsacks cover'd with dust!)
The blood of the city up—arm'd! arm'd!

This shocking boosterism is notable for its lack of identifying personal features. The soldiers have brown faces. That's it. D. H. Lawrence complained about Whitman's women that they "needn't have had faces at all." It's true of these soldiers, as it is true of Whitman's first war poems: generic, anonymous, unlived, a visual spectacle.

Whitman showed up rather late to the war. On Tuesday, December 16, 1862, he found in the *New York Herald* a list of soldiers from the 51st New York Infantry who'd been killed or wounded at the first battle of Fredericksburg. Among the names was "First Lieutenant G. W. Whitmore, Company D," which Whitman rightly deduced as his brother George's misspelled name. The poet took fifty dollars, which his mother withdrew from savings, traveled south by train to the nation's capital and then by boat to Aquia Landing and finally Falmouth, Virginia. (In Philadephia, while changing train cars, he had his pocket picked and then showed up in D.C., as he wrote, "without a dime.")

George was not among the thousands in the huge hospital tent-camps around the capital. Instead, Walt found him nursing a shrapnel-wound to the cheek at a makeshift hospital along the Rappahannock, near the battle. Here he tended his brother, who returned to fight in other battles, heroically, rising to the rank of Captain.

George went back to war but Walt did not go back to New York. Was it a political magnet that drew Whitman back to D.C.? (After all, he said the role of poet is "representative.") Was it some paternal-maternal need to take custody of so many desperately needful boys?

The hospital camps around the city were huge, tens of thousands of wounded at times, and they were horrible in stench and disease, offering grim prospects of recovery. Infection killed more than artillery. Walt's own first sight of a hospital camp was, as he wrote to his mother, "a heap of feet, arms, legs, &c. under a tree." Was his compulsion to stay erotic, medical, aesthetic?

Here is what I know. He worked at government jobs, as a clerk, as a copyist, even getting fired at one point when a midlevel administrator deduced he was the author of that obscene book *Leaves of Grass*. He walked the city, he nodded to Lincoln who sometimes passed by, and over four years he made "more than six hundred visits to hospitals, tending, he claimed, to '80,000 to 100,000 of the wounded and sick, as sustainer of spirit and body in some degree.'" He was nurse and doctor, he was secretary and last rites-giver, he was friend and companion to thousands. He worked a few hours a day, then went to the camps with his pockets full of stamps, crackers, horehound candy, pennies, lemons and oranges, jars of pudding, paper and pens, needle and thread. One hot day in the middle of June, he spent a chunk of salary to buy a wagonload of ice cream to soothe the boys of Carver Hospital. He read to them in large groups. The letters he wrote back to their families will break your heart. He sent news, death notices, requests, sometimes just to say *I held his hand*, or *wiped his face*, or *cleaned his bandages*. Sometimes just to say, *I was there*. To the parents of Erastus Haskell he wrote: "he . . . behaved always correct & decent . . . I used to sit on the side of the bed—I said once, You don't talk any, Erastus, you leave me to do all the talking—he only answered quietly, I was never much of a talker." Erastus languished for nearly a year and died of typhus: "he had his hair cut close about ten or twelve days before he died."

Here is what he did. He got his hands bloody. He got his hands on these hurt soldiers one at a time. He learned their names; he nursed and aided them. Whitman replaced sight with touch—that most intimate of senses, but also the most dirty.

How is death sane? The root of "sanity" is the Latin word *sanitas*. Thus, my dirty little secret: This same word serves as the root for "sanitary." To be sane is to be clean. To be healthy is to be reasonable.

This sounds like the perfect formula for an America, in the 1840s and 50s, wild for progress and perfection, hungry for spas and cures, just discovering things like bacteria and germs. The war dirtied our hands, our minds, and our very sense of ourselves as a nation.

The war poems Whitman wrote during and after his hospital experiences are quite different from his prior ones. And he wrote a great deal during this decade. As Kim Roberts notes, "During his time in Washington (from the age of 44 to 54), Whitman wrote *Drum-Taps* (published in 1865), *Democratic Vistas* (1871), *Passage to India* (1871), and prepared two new editions of *Leaves of Grass* (1867 and 1871). He wrote drafts of material that would eventually become the basis for his books *Memoranda during the War* (1875), and *Specimen Days and Collect* (1882). It was an extremely prolific period that resulted in almost one hundred new poems." But documenting the hospitals was as urgent to Whitman as his poetry, as he attests: "the Hospital part of the drama . . . deserves indeed to be recorded . . . over the whole land . . . an unending, universal mourning-wail of women, parents, orphans—the marrow of the tragedy concentrated in those Hospitals."

The "Hospital part of the drama" infuses his poems with a particularity uncommon in his earlier War poems. Now he describes "bearing the bandages, water and sponge, / Straight and swift to my wounded I go . . . / Where their priceless blood reddens the grass on the ground." Here in "The Wound-Dresser," only a hands-on participant would know to say "from the stump of the arm, the amputated hand, / I undo the clotted lint, remove the slough, wash off the matter and blood." And the portraits in the second half of *Drum-Taps* are not collective, nor generic: a poem for two veterans, a tan-faced prairie boy, one soldier, one "camerado" at a time.

The movement of Whitman's imagination is a movement through the transcendental toward the real. It mirrors the blurred, optimistic youth of a country going through a phase of brutal growth. It took the vicious fact of war—getting his hands dirty, touching things, one at a time, not just looking at them—to show Whitman the insanity of experience.

Death may be sane, but life is not. Death is perfection, it is peace, it is clarity. Life is the horror. This discovery is the deepest "vision" at the heart of the lilac elegy:

> I saw battle-corpses, myriads of them,
> And the white skeletons of young men, I saw them,
> I saw the debris and debris of all the slain soldiers of the war,
> But I saw they were not as was thought,
> They themselves were fully at rest, they suffer'd not,
> The living remain'd and suffer'd, the mother suffer'd,
> And the wife and the child and the musing comrade suffer'd,
> And the armies that remain'd suffer'd.

So let me clarify. It is not that Whitman learned, in the war, the importance of touch. And he has always known that transcendence requires a death. In "This Compost," he praises the "foul liquid and meat" of the dead, the "distemper'd corpses" that have startled him on his walk through the "still woods." "Perhaps every mite has once form'd part of a sick person," he says, incredulous with the discovery that even the "resurrection of the wheat" has been fed by the fetid "corruptions" of death. "What chemistry!" he exclaims, that the result of the natural process should be "that all is clean forever and ever." This poem appears under its present title in the first post-War edition of *Leaves of Grass*, in 1867, as part of the *Drum-Taps* section, where its narrative placement suggests the war dead. But a much earlier version appeared in *Leaves* as early as 1856 as "Poem of Wonder at the Resurrection of the Wheat," and seems to have been about a decaying animal in a field.

In "Crossing Brooklyn Ferry," Whitman again moves from sight to the particularity of touch. This poem appeared first as "The Sun-Down Poem" in the 1856 *Leaves*. Here, he "receiv[es] identity by [his] body." His skin itself—that particular "necessary film"—verifies his "nighest name" and provides the necessary means of contact, connecting one to another: "I . . . felt their arms on my neck as a stood, or the negligent leaning of their flesh against me as I sat." Only through this particularity—of touch, of nomination and identity—is Whitman's vision of hope and soulful improvement possible.

"Is this then a touch?" he asks as early as 1855 in "Song of Myself." This great poem also started with sight, but here, at the poem's heart, it is touch, he says, "quivering me to a new identity." It is, he says, "about as much as I can stand." Touch is unclean but generative, it is particular but connective, it is an individual's act that nonetheless transfers sensations—those real thoughts—from one to another in a type of literal transcendence.

Yet this is one thing in theory, in abstraction, in "Song of Myself" or "Crossing Brooklyn Ferry." It is another thing entirely to be confronted with the fact of a presidential hero shot in the head and the beseeching voices and ripped-apart bodies of so many young soldiers dying one by one. Is it possible that Whitman invents a form of transcendentalism that accommodates the real? Maybe this is Whitman's greatest thematic contribution: not that the Civil War provided him with his first real validation of the necessity of touch; erotic, but also erosive, touch's power has been part of his scheme all along. Rather now, touch—the knowledge of bodies—is made human, is given exact names, faces, and bloody hands by the War and by his transformative experiences at the hospitals. Whitman learned that touch may bring erotic delight and power, but it also brings damage, loss, and pain. Thus the lilac elegy becomes his great "retrievement out of the night."

So here we are at the end of the beginning. And here is Whitman back in "Song of Myself," always already ahead of us on the open road. When he says we can look for him under our boot-soles, he also says that he will "filter and fibre [our] blood." We may still be looking, seeing. But he has made the progressive evolution to touch: the innermost kind of touch. He is literally inside us, touching us there—touching our blood, cleaning it, filtering and fibering it, as in a medical procedure to come. This is Whitman's vision, the hoped-for evolution toward a perfect life, him and our one-self, all of us together, sane and sacred at the end.

Whitman's Compost

Stanley Plumly

The day Abraham Lincoln was first elected President, the Prince of Wales (later King Edward VII) arrived in Washington to find, in the words of a British reporter, a "strange city, whose streets of ill-built houses connect to the most noble public buildings" or, as an American writer puts it, in the same year, "Washington was merely a place for government. It was an idea set in a wilderness." If Washington, in 1860, was set in a wilderness, it was, worst of all, in itself a bit of a wilderness set in a wilderness. That is to say, it was a swamp, a mud city, a sort of enormous farm lot, a place where pigs and cattle and a few wild things generally roamed freely over the landscape and the "cityscape" and where dysentery and diarrhea were common and where, until the Civil War broke out, saloons and brothels and gambling halls outnumbered anything approaching culture. Yet once the war did break out and brought its carnage home, the low-life establishments were largely replaced by no more or less than tent hospitals, bivouac avenues, crowds of mixed loyalties, piles of body parts, and graves. The pigs and the mud, however, remained.

The Capitol Dome had still to be built and the Washington Monument was only halfway up and resembled a tall factory chimney. And to complement the herds of pigs and cattle, "everywhere hucksters abounded," writes Margaret Leech in her classic *Reveille in Washington*: "Fish and oyster peddlers cried their wares and tooted their horns on the corners. Flocks of geese waddled on Pennsylvania Avenue. . . . People emptied slops and refuse in the gutters." And Washington was certainly the poor cousin to Philadelphia and New York, older cities to the north, with its limited economy of government clerks, a few farmers, fishermen, bakers, and carpenters, and, by one accounting, in 1860, three veterinarians, six undertakers, a hundred doctors, and, naturally, a hundred-and-eighty lawyers. A provincial capital, a city betwixt and between, Washington, in its way, was a compromise city, with a Southern soul.

Compare it to mid-century, "mast-hemm'd Manhattan," for instance, and there is no comparison. "I am quite fond," writes peripatetic poet Walt Whitman, at the early stages of the Civil War, while he is still living in Brooklyn—"I am quite fond of crossing on the Fulton Ferry, or South Ferry, between Brooklyn and New York, on the big handsome boats. They run continually day and night. I know most of the pilots, and I go up on deck and stay as long as I choose. The scene is very curious and full of variety. The shipping along the wharves looks like a forest of bare trees. Then there are all classes of sailing vessels and steamers, some of the most beautiful steamships in the world, going or coming from Europe, or on the California route, all these on the move." This scene, of course, has already been elevated to transcendent status in "Crossing Brooklyn Ferry" five years earlier. It's a scene that makes Washington feel like the frontier.

Whitman doesn't make it to the Washington area until late in 1862, when the city has been relatively transformed from general muck and mess into a more specific yet massive muck and mess of hospitals and encampments. Whitman's brother George is into his second enlistment in the Brooklyn Regiment of the Army of the Potomac and has just been involved in the Second Battle of Bull Run, located loosely between Manassas and Fredericksburg, Virginia, less than a good day's march from Washington. George has not, however, been heard from for a while—and he is an inveterate letter writer. Fearing the worst, Whitman makes his way south to see what the story is. After a stopover in Washington, he heads to the expanse of the battlefield and its makeshift hospitals, where, in fact, he does find George wounded, but not seriously.

It is widely assumed that Whitman spent all of his time in Washington, tending the wounded and acting as parental or fraternal patron. And it's true that most of his ten-year exile from his beloved Brooklyn was spent in Washington, but not all of it and not at the beginning. When Whitman finds George he finds a calling. Once he witnesses the lack of care and the degree of despair among soldiers hardly more than boys, he becomes committed to doing what he can for them, whether through nursing, counseling, or letter-writing for those unable to do it themselves. But it all starts, not in Washington, but on the battlefield, right there in Falmouth, Virginia, outside Fredericksburg, down the road from the original year-old Battle of Bull Run.

"I hurriedly went down to the field of war in Virginia," he writes on December 13th; on December 21st, he begins "my visits among the camp hospitals of the Army of the Potomac." And as the December days pass, "spent a good part of the day in a brick mansion on the banks of the Rappahannock, used as a hospital since the battle; seems to have received the worst cases." One of those days, being the good reporter that he is, he notices, "at the foot of a tree, within ten yards of the front of the house . . . a heap of amputated feet, legs, arms, etc.—a full load for a one-horse cart." On another day, "several dead bodies lie near, each covered in a brown woolen blanket. In the dooryard, towards the river, are fresh graves, mostly of officers, their names on pieces of barrel staves or broken boards stuck in dirt."

These moments fairly represent samples of what Whitman would begin to see on a daily basis. More than the hard fact of the facts, though, is the texture of what he's experiencing—the flesh and blood of it, the utter ephemeral mortal nature of it, the makeshift quality of absolute mortality. Even when he establishes residence in Washington, he ranges out into the fields of dead and wounded after battle, sometimes following along with the transport of survivors back into the city. And as well as his roles as self-designated nurse and confessor to and for these broken young men, once he is back in Washington, Whitman also becomes their aide-de-camp, when he can manage it. "I try to give a word or trifle to every one without exception. . . . I make regular rounds among them all. I give all kinds of sustenance, blackberries, peaches, lemons & sugar, wines . . . shirts & all articles of underclothing. . . . I always give paper, envelopes, stamps. . . . To many I give (when I have it) small sums of money—half the soldiers have not a cent."

Drum-Taps is the large group of poems that comes out of these years: a good many of them drawn directly from the Virginia fields of the harvest of the lost and almost lost, "Vigil Strange I Kept on the Field One Night," "The Wound Dresser," "A Sight in Camp in the Daybreak Gray and Dim," and the wonderful postcard-size poems such as "Cavalry Crossing a Ford" and "By Bivouac's Fitful Flame." All the war poems are beautifully observed, accurately rendered, passionately felt. Each of them, in its own way, keeps vigil, marches in the ranks on a road unknown, on a "route through a heavy wood with muffled steps in the darkness." They all see "shadows of the deepest, deepest black." Whitman will spend these several war years working poorly paying jobs in order to support not only himself but his constant visits to the various hospitals, visits that after 1863 become central to his Washington residence. By 1864, "saturated with the virus of the hospitals"—as one of his doctors puts it—Whitman himself becomes one of the wounded, "having too deeply imbibed poison into his system." What exactly is ailing him is not clear, but exhaustion combined with exposure cannot have helped. Nor can the emotional toll be discounted. He is forty-five now, with twenty-eight more years to live the compromised life of a veteran.

As a coda to *Drum-Taps*, Whitman's great Civil War elegy for Lincoln and the nation closes the book on his personal connection to the tragedy and its consequences but not on his afterlife in Washington. He'll hang on in the recovering city until 1873, occupying different posts for the government, moving from one job to another, usually because of *Leaves of Grass*. Health juxtaposed in a slant rhyme with death has been a subtext in Whitman early on in his writing. Death and thought of death have been, like the broken soldiers, his long companions. The health of death has been that part of him that likely pulled him into his sense of mission in the hospitals. Yet the same year he writes "Crossing Brooklyn Ferry," his visionary masterpiece of life as afterlife, he writes as well his poem of cosmic vision entitled "This Compost," in which he imagines the whole planet as a compost heap of dead animal, vegetable, mineral, and, ultimately, human flesh. "I will not touch my flesh to the earth," he says as if in fear of contagion. "O how can it be that the ground itself does not sicken?" He then spends quite a few of the next lines listing the "blood of herbs, roots, orchards, grains" and the "foul meat" just under the surface as his evidence. The graphic in Whitman is often underrated, and here, in this palpably corporeal poem, there's a certain fascination with the vile vulnerability yet putrid virility of the earth. Now the poem turns, as if Whitman's divided mind needs to redress its balance, its equilibrium: so in its second half Whitman extols what he is seeing and imagining. "Behold this compost! behold it well!" And the pun on "well"—as the antithesis of sickness—seems to me no verbal accident. He takes the word "compost" and in a stroke fills out its implication of an enriching reality: without death and burial there can be no "resurrection of the wheat . . . no new-born life . . . no lilacs blooming in the dooryards." "What chemistry!" he exclaims. And for the rest of the poem the earth is alive with spring and summer and "the transparent green-wash of the sea." At this point the poem becomes Whitman's unconscious preparation for a war that has been rumored for years.

By the end of the poem, Whitman's vision, as always, is all-embracing. In the last lines, he speaks forgivingly of the paradox of life in death, death in life. Indeed, he speaks lovingly. "Now I am terrified at the Earth. . . . It grows such sweet things out of such corruptions, / It turns harmless and stainless on its axis, with such endless successions of diseas'd corpses, / It distills such exquisite winds out of such fetor, / It renews with such unwitting looks its prodigal, annual, sumptuous crops, / It gives such divine materials to men, and accepts such leavings from them at last." It cannot be too difficult to pick out in this panorama the small particular faces of those young men Whitman watched die even as he ministered to their health.

The Self in the Poem

Linda Gregerson

> Through you I shall be born again; myself again and again; myself without others; myself with a tomb; myself beyond death. I imagine you taking my name; I imagine you saying "myself myself" again and again. And suddenly there will be no blue sky or sun or shape of anything without that simple utterance.
>
> . . .
>
> Sometimes when I wander in these woods whose prince I am, I hear a voice and know that I am not alone.
>
> . . .
>
> Solemn truths! Lucid inescapable foolishness! None of that for me. To be the salt of Walt, oceanic in osteality! . . . The fruit of the tomb! The flute of the tomb! The loot of gloom!

These words do not hail from the mouth of Walt Whitman directly. They are the words of one of his most astute heirs and readers: Mark Strand. Or rather, they are the words of a book called *The Monument*, Strand's monument to the egotistical sublime. They are the words of poetry spoken in prose. Or rather, they are the words of the poet's "translator in the future," through whose hands the poet's prose appears to have passed before reaching us, his readers. That translator, and we readers, thus find ourselves conjured into perpetual service at the votive flame of one who channels the one who aspired to have changed forever the possibilities of poetic speech. The satire is a little wicked, but the conceit is penetrating.

Walt Whitman did change forever the possibilities of American poetic speech: he enabled American poetry to leap quite over the Victoriana that so beautifully elaborated, and stultified, English lyric production right into the thick of the First World War. In *The Monument*, Strand is not merely burlesquing Whitman—and who could possibly outdo the poet himself on the scale of outrageousness?—he is dissecting the central rhetorical vehicle of Whitman's art: the self so large, so exemplary, so all-encompassing that it empties itself of all specific content and becomes tautology. This despite the epic catalogues—full to bursting with bodies and place names and bustle and tools of the many trades—that constitute Whitman's other most-often-resorted-to device.

The Civil War marked a dramatic turning point in Whitman's poetry as in his life. The grandiosity and over-inflation, the heady idealizations of manual labor by one who preferred to "loaf," all this encountered a terrific dose of reality in the regimental encampments of Virginia and the hospital wards of wartime Washington. *Drum-Taps*, bravely, foolishly, wonderfully, records the double consciousness, the no-holds-barred before and after: both the thumping boosterism of "Beat! Beat! Drums," "First O Songs for a Prelude," and "Song of the Banner at Daybreak" and the utterly different portraits of "A Sigt in Camp in the Daybreak Gray and Dim," "Cavalry Crossing a Ford," and "Bivouac on a Mountain Side," poems suddenly shocked into sobriety, plain denotation, and, utterly new to Whitman, understatement.

> Three forms I see on stretchers lying, brought out there
> untended lying,
> Over each the blanket spread, ample brownish woolen blanket,
> Gray and heavy blanket, folding, covering all.
> ("A Sight in Camp in the Daybreak Gray and Dim")

The sentences are simpler and shorter in these newer poems. The images are local—"the bandages, water, and sponge"—before they are required to be exemplary. Some of the poems themselves are only four or five or six lines long.

A less confident poet might have tried to suppress the evidence of those earlier, ignorant calls-to-war. A less confident man might have tried to over-explain. But only a single poem in *Drum-Taps*,

"The Wound-Dresser," allows itself a revisionary backward look:

> (Arous'd and angry, I'd thought to beat the alarum, and urge
> relentless war,
> But soon my fingers fail'd me, my face droop'd and I resign'd myself
> To sit by the wounded and soothe them, or silently watch
> the dead;) . . .
> Of those armies so rapid so wondrous what saw you to tell us?
> What stays with you latest and deepest? . . .
>
> I dress the perforated shoulder, the foot with the bullet-wound,
> Cleanse the one with a gnawing and putrid gangrene, so sickening
> so offensive,
> While the attendant stands behind aside me holding the tray and
> pail.

Aroused and angry he had been, in 1861, at the breaking of the Union and the firing on Fort Sumter. But he had also been an enthusiastic supporter of the war with Mexico fifteen years earlier, the war of U.S. aggression that so horrified Emerson and James Russell Lowell. Until he spent those harrowing months attending to the wounded in Washington, Whitman saw militarism as a great tonic antidote to everything that afflicted American manhood, especially the debilitating absorption in commerce, or getting and spending.

The mythology that grew up around Walt Whitman, both during his lifetime and in subsequent eras, has invested heavily in the intertwining of life and work. He was the great visionary of democracy and emancipation, and is credited, with reason, for instinctive recoil against slavery. But he was never an abolitionist, despite his reverence for Lincoln: in the pages of the *Brooklyn Daily Eagle*, he excoriated abolitionists as "foolish red-hot fanatics" and abolitionism as "impracticable" and "wild." He had written in his notebooks:

> I am the poet of slaves and of the masters of slaves . . .

I go with the slaves of the earth equally with the masters
And I will stand between the masters and the slaves,
Entering into both so that both shall understand me alike.

But in the *Brooklyn Daily Times* he wrote: "Who believes that Whites and Blacks can ever amalgamate in America? Or who wishes it to happen? Nature has set an impassable seal against it. Besides, is not America for the Whites? And is it not better so?" We like to think that Whitman's heart was better than his head for politics, that, in the brother-to-brother encounter, his extraordinary aptitude for natural sympathy was a touchstone to be relied upon. But here is what he writes about watching the soldiers of the First Regiment, U.S. Colored Troops, receive their pay: "Occasionally, but not often, there are some thoroughly African physiognomies, very black in color, large protruding lips, low forehead, etc. But I have to say that I do not see one utterly revolting face." And when, the following spring, he watched five black regiments march in review with the rest of Burnside's army, "It looked funny," he wrote, "to see the President standing with his hat off to them just the same as the rest." Compare this to the "polish'd and perfect limbs" of the laboring Negro in "Song of Myself."

Why rehearse these painful anomalies in an extraordinary writer's extraordinary affective and cognitive embrace? We are all historical actors: the insights and assumptions that constitute our own moral bearing will surely, a hundred years from now, be found severely wanting, will produce some shudders in even those who wish our memories well. Whitman's editorials on race and his casual comments on the black Union regiments bitterly disappoint us, wound us even, and their power to wound is fresh. I mention them because they shock us into thinking, once again, about what it means to read historically. I mention them because I struggle with them myself as I try to read Walt Whitman and understand his place in America's imagination of itself. I mention them because, once again, the poets of America, or many of them, are struggling with what it means to speak both of and beyond the self, to write, in other words, politically.

Whitman's aestheticizations—magnanimous and conflicted,

encompassing and appropriative, visionary and vicarious in equal measure—are always, in Michael Warner's wonderful phrase, the products of a "richly disorganized consciousness." Nowhere, perhaps, is that rich disorganization more vividly manifested than in the poet's visitations at the bedsides of working-class young men and soldiers. These began when he was still in New York and hitching rides with omnibus drivers. Visiting the ill and injured men in Broadway Hospital, he catalogued their afflictions in a series of articles for the *New York Leader*: fractured bones and amputations, gunshot wounds, burns and scaldings, rheumatism, typhoid, bronchitis, consumption, delirium tremens, dysentery, pneumonia, opium overdose. After war had been declared, Broadway Hospital began to fill up with soldiers who had joined their regiments in New York only to be felled by a measles epidemic. Subsequently, of course, Whitman's ministrations to the ill and wounded in Washington's wartime hospitals became the defining experience of his life in the nation's capital. He assisted at surgeries, brought gifts of jelly and tobacco, socks and shirts, read to the patients, wrote letters for them, fed them, fanned them, sat with them in their death throes. He had written: "I believe a leaf of grass is no less than the journeywork of the stars, / And the pismire is equally perfect, and a grain of sand, and the egg of the wren." He had written: "I do not press my finger across my mouth, / I keep as delicate around the bowels as around the head and heart." These principled inclusions were put severely to the test in the wartime hospital wards, where the smells of diarrhea and gangrenous limbs, the sight of the surgical buckets and fouled bed linens, the sounds of human beings in pain and delirium, would prove too much for many a well-meaning visitor. Squeamishness, false delicacy, disgust were moral failings of the first order in Whitman's universe and, infinitely to his credit, he refused to admit them.

It is not entirely true, of course, that Whitman never pressed his finger across his mouth. When John Addington Symonds, a deep admirer of the Calamus poems, wrote a carefully worded letter inquiring further into Whitman's thoughts about "the love of man for man," Whitman wrote back in high dudgeon about these "morbid inferences—wh' are disavow'd by me & seem damnable." He was "as hostile to sexual inversion," wrote a disappointed Symonds, "as any law-abiding humdrum Anglo-Saxon could desire." If Whitman's intimate ministrations in the hospital wards seem less than utterly disinterested to us now, if the rounds of mercy, with their interwoven strands of frankness and occlusion, seem more complexly motivated than hagiography has allowed, these tensions and embargos are inseparable from their urgency, and are kin—though never a simple key—to the urgency of the poems.

The strategic cordonings-off of New Criticism offered a crucial corrective to the sentimental conflations of earlier biographical criticism; the strategic disavowals of Language Poetry, or rather, of its manifestos, offered a timely antidote to the inertias of latter day confessionalism. But neither affords a fully sufficient model for reading. The wish to construe a self "behind" the poem is one of the persistent engines to reading, as "story" is one of the most persistent units of human comprehension. The gestures of self and the lineaments of story: for resilience and momentum and, yes, for subversive possibility, one would be hard pressed to find poetic instruments with richer aptitude. The longing for familiar kinds of meaning, in other words, is unkillable. It is also, crucially, ripe for transformation. So the built self, the simultaneous invitation to and refusal of biographical reading, has the power to lure both reader and writer into genuine discovery. We discard it at our peril. We trust it at our peril.

As an ordinary rule of thumb, one cannot hold a writer responsible for the excesses of his followers and champions. But Whitman was also an eager orchestrator of his own mythology. This goes beyond the notorious strategies for self-promotion: the writing of anonymous auto-reviews, the flat-out lies about print runs and sales figures, the conversion of a private letter from Emerson into the gold-leaf letters of blazon on the cover of *Leaves of Grass*. It includes as well Whitman's boasts about the "magnetism" he spread like balm in the hospital wards, the stoking of adulation, the basking in euphemistically unified accounts of his life and opinions. In this one respect we must do better for Whitman than Whitman has done for himself. It was when he brazenly embraced his own disharmonies—"Do I contradict myself? / Very well then I contradict myself"—that Whitman offered the truest key to the originality of his contribution. He construed his voice as a public voice, a voice that was capacious enough to "contain multitudes." The very exorbitance of the poetic instrument is the key to its cunning. And as Strand's faceless *Monument* reminds us, that instrument depends, for its cunning and its plausibility alike, as much upon what it omits as upon what it includes.

What it omits is what we are enjoined to provide. "I might not tell everybody, but I will tell you," he wrote, in a poem addressed to every you who would listen. "All I mark as my own you shall offset it with your own / Else it were time lost listening to me." These are extraordinary rhetorical postulates, entirely aware of their own paradoxical nature. Whitman contrived to speak with unprecedented intimacy in unprecedentedly public terms: for sheer communal reach, the classical epics were as nothing to the *Leaves of Grass*. His performance of public confidence was nowhere more outrageous than in its insistence on private confiding. And the insistence is a two-way proposition. That reading should be an act of self-discovery in the strong sense, which is to say, self-making (very far from the sentimental exercise we think of as self-discovery today), is a venerable rhetorical proposition. What was new in Whitman were the lengths to which he was willing to go in daring his reader into reciprocity. Invoking the lineaments of selfhood—my body, my appetites, my paths across the pavements and the countryside—Whitman is partly conceding to a common mode of making sense and partly seeking to explode it forever. We mistake the proposition altogether if we filter out the dissonant parts or construe the categories as naive. The self Walt Whitman demands we imagine by means of the poem is the self we would be were we whole.

Whitman in Baghdad

Ann Townsend

"I was going to hold forth on arms, and the violence of warfare, in a meter suited to the manner," wrote the Roman poet Ovid at the outset of his *Amores*; "but Cupid, laughing," he continued, "stole one foot from the second line," shifting the meter out of the heroic hexameters used by Virgil in his *Aeneid* and into elegiac couplets, thereby lightening the line into one more "suited to the manner" of love poetry. In antiquity, the meter matters when poets speak of kissing rather than of killing. Ovid's sly invocation of Cupid alerts his readers: only a slim line separates erotic poetry and war poetry. The two modes have more in common than we might think. Poets craft their singular versions of history by choosing which stories to tell. But how we tell the story matters, too: the poetic modes and genres we use when we write, as Ovid knew, change everything.

The difference between writing in the heroic manner, itself an idealized and elevated mode for depicting war's visceral brutality, and writing in the direct, ground-level present tense of first person experience is in fact the difference between writing the epic and the lyric poem. Today, the subject of war continues to compel, though the meter has changed. Think of Yusef Komunyakaa, of Bruce Weigl, and, more recently, of Brian Turner. But think, too, of the poet whose war took place right here at home. Though Walt Whitman never picked up a rifle, he saw at first hand the catastrophic aftermath of what bullets and cannons can do to a man.

Say you are twenty years old. Say your father died and you felt cut adrift. Say, as Richard Hugo does, your life broke down. This is my brother's story. On March 20th, 2003, the United States First Marine Expeditionary Force drove its tanks through the center of Iraq, along Highway One, destination Baghdad. My youngest brother had joined the Marines in a fit of indecision about his future. My father, who died when my brother was thirteen years old, had served as a Marine stateside in between the Korean and Vietnam wars. My brother wanted to follow, somehow, in his path. I don't think he ever imagined he would find himself on the front line of a full-scale invasion.

During that week in March of 2003, other military divisions raced up the major highways across Iraq, from every part of the country, aiming to converge in Baghdad. My brother's First Marine Division fought its way to the eastern side of Baghdad, and then launched a successful attack on the city itself. These were both exciting and terrifying days for a young man who had, up until that point, led a safe and even sheltered life. After the early, chaotic, months of the war had passed, my brother was assigned to the Camp Whitehorse detention facility outside of the city of Nasiriyah, about two hundred miles south of Baghdad. Like the notorious Abu Ghraib prison, Camp Whitehorse was a prisoner-of-war camp run by American soldiers. They had little training and almost no support. In modern warfare, technology has given us the capacity to kill at a distance. But we must tend our captured enemies, as well as our wounded comrades, all too closely.

What did my brother see in Iraq? All the evidence says that he saw too much. He himself will not say. What did Whitman see during the Civil War? In his case, we have an extensive and detailed record. Whitman recorded his Civil War experiences in a series of notebooks and letters, and in the poems of *Drum-Taps*. These poems record Whitman's evolution from the man first filled with patriotic fervor, to the witness shocked by the ruined bodies of the wounded, to, at last, the nurse with an abiding compassion and love for the soldiers under his careful ministrations. By the conclusion of *Drum-Taps*, Whitman's poems have begun to question the dream of America's expansive promise amid the young nation's faltering democratic present.

Whitman's direct experience of the consequences of war changed his poems. While the early poems in *Drum-Taps* identify with, albeit at a distance, the beautiful young soldiers leaving New York for battle, the empathy evident in the later poems only emerges after having experienced ground-level interaction with these men and their actual bodies. The difference between Whitman's earlier and later poems is the difference between imagining the heroic body and witnessing the wounded, convalescent body. In "A March in the Ranks Hard-Press't, and the Road Unknown," the speaker enters a church that has been reconfigured as a field hospital, and sees

> . . . a sight beyond all the pictures and poems ever made,
> Shadows of deepest, deepest black, just lit by moving candles and lamps,
> And by one great pitchy torch, stationary, with wild red flame, and clouds of smoke,
> By these, crowds, groups of forms, vaguely I see, on the floor, some in the pews laid down,
> At my feet more distinctly, a soldier, a mere lad, in danger of bleeding to death. . . .

Whitman's speaker attempts to staunch the flow of blood, and then looks, again, all around:

> . . . I sweep my eyes o'er the scene, fain to absorb it all,
> Faces, varieties, postures beyond description, most in obscurity, some of them dead,
> Surgeons operating, attendants holding lights, the smell of ether, the odor of blood,
> The crowd, O the crowd of the bloody forms of soldiers—the yard outside also fill'd,
> Some on the bare ground, some on planks or stretchers, some in the death-spasm sweating,
> An occasional scream or cry, the doctor's shouted orders or calls;
> The glisten of the little steel instruments catching the glint of the torches,
> These I resume as I chant, I see again the forms, I smell the odor,
> Then hear outside the orders given, *Fall in; my men, fall in;*
> But first I bend to the dying lad, his eyes open, a half-smile

gives he me,
Then the eyes close, calmly close, and I speed forth to the darkness,
Resuming, marching, ever in darkness marching, on in the ranks,
The unknown road still marching.

When we are ill or injured, when we convalesce, we occupy a shadow land. We rest at a crossroads, the two roads, as Elaine Scarry says, leading in very different directions. Our bodies are inexorably fragile. The damaged body is in flux, occupying a middle ground, not quite healthy, not yet dead. Those damaged by war, but not killed, whether soldiers or noncombatants, often simply disappear, their stories untold. The words we write about them occupy a similar in-between land; the outcome of the story we tell has not yet been determined. But these words keep the soldier in view, grant him his own agency, and prevent at least one particular life from disappearing altogether.

One of the implicit questions of the later poems in *Drum-Taps* is: What to do with the wounded body? Do we praise it? Bury it? Do we keep it alive by writing it down? Whitman immersed himself in this shadow land, committed himself to the writing of it. In a letter to Ralph Waldo Emerson, he reports that the young soldiers in the hospitals have revealed to him a new world, "a world full of its separate action, play, suggestiveness—surely a medium world, advanced between our well-known practised one of body and of mind. . . ." Perhaps, then, it is no surprise that during this time Whitman also grew interested in the more fugitive medical phenomena he encountered, such as, Robert Leigh Davis reports, "the phantom limb, which is both real and illusory, both physical and ghost-like." In these poems, the meditative language is itself a medium, a middle ground, a locus for something like Keatsian negative capability. Language intervenes and mediates between consciousness and the object under scrutiny; descriptive words help us to absorb the unthinkable.

But it is also human to fear the boundaries that separate one body from another. Jean Paul Sartre could as easily be speaking of blood when he says, about the stickiness of honey, "The viscous is a state half-way between solid and liquid . . . it is unstable but it does not flow. . . ." For Sartre, plunging a hand into honey is quite a different experience from placing his hand into water. In water, he says, "I remain a solid. But to touch stickiness is to risk diluting myself into viscosity." As I say, he could as easily be speaking of the properties of blood, and I think of Whitman, who bandaged, cleaned, staunched bleeding wounds, who encountered all manner of human stickiness. Whitman's poem "The Wound Dresser" meditates on this interaction. Just as the men in "A March in the Ranks Hard-Press't, and the Road Unknown" must continue to march onward, the narrator in "The Wound Dresser" can only bear the consistent awfulness of what he sees by going forward. The wound dresser makes his rounds among the injured and convalescing soldiers. He says "to each and all one after another I draw near, not one do I miss, / An attendant follows holding a tray, he carries a refuse pail, / Soon to be filled with clotted rags and blood, emptied, and fill'd again. / . . . I onward go. . . ." In this poem, every body he encounters is breaking or broken, and all he can do is "pacify them with a soothing hand."

Elaine Scarry, in *The Body in Pain*, gets to the heart of the matter: "The main purpose and outcome of war is injuring." This fact "may disappear from view simply by being omitted: one can read many pages of a historic or strategic account of a particular military campaign, or listen to many successive installments in a newscast narrative of events in a contemporary war, without encountering the acknowledgment that the purpose of the event described is to alter (to burn, to blast, to shell, to cut) human tissue." Why do we write about the wounded in war? Because people themselves, as well as their experiences, disappear. Because the individual stories of thousands of soldiers, young and far from home, are never recorded. Or: are told only in the sweeping histories that blur and erase individual suffering and action. So it is all the more necessary that, when we are faced with the unbearable, we do not look away. Walt Whitman understood that "extraordinary circumstances should breed extraordinary acts of empathy."

In one of his many war notebooks, Whitman writes, "The expression of American personality through this war is not to be looked for in the great campaign, and the battle-fights. It is to be looked for . . . in the hospitals, among the wounded." Years after the war, Whitman wrote, "Curious as it may seem the War, to me, proved humanity." Away from home, immersed instead in the culture of illness and recovery, Whitman turned away from the poetry of expansive joy and integration. Away from family, away from permanent work and a defined position in society, Whitman writes some of his most intimate and humane poems. The later poems in *Drum-Taps* represent the war experience not by invoking national pride or the epic achievement of battle, but by immersing the speaker in the midst of the sensory and emotional nightmare that follows the battle itself.

In 2004, my brother returned from his war. What he saw he will not say. What he did he will not tell: I know only the most bare and impersonal outlines. Stationed at Camp Whitehorse, he was asked to guard and care for all manner of men, from thieves to boys, to bombers, to those imprisoned because they were injured and had nowhere else to go. The conditions were cruel, the barracks blisteringly hot, the prisoners living at times in open-air pens, without sufficient water or food. Some of the soldiers there were willing to do nearly anything to extract confessions from those they interrogated. One day, perhaps after witnessing a particularly brutal interrogation, my brother could not continue. His body, itself, simply broke down. His commanding officer reluctantly shipped him back to the United States. He was hospitalized, for a short time, then, astonishingly, put back into uniform, and ordered to report for duty. And so he returned, as did thousands of other young men and women.

Years after these events, my brother looks forward, not back. While writing this essay, I learned about the brutalities and deaths that took place at Camp Whitehorse, and about the base closing and the court-martials that eventually followed. I learned these things not from him, but from an internet search. Unsurprisingly, only the barest outlines remain, the process of erasure having already begun. Long ago, Ovid argued that when we write about love, we must borrow and adapt means and methods from our brother warriors. The distinction between love poetry and war poetry is narrow indeed. A shift in perspective, an understanding that the epic gesture is unavailable to us now, the accidental loss of a poetic foot: the poetry of witness has more in common with love poetry than one silent warrior might ever imagine.

Emily Dickinson

AT HOME WITH EMILY DICKINSON

Wings

Stanley Plumly

Emily Dickinson brings up birds in some two hundred and twenty of her roughly eighteen hundred poems. Mostly she mentions them as contributions to the texture: as an analogue, a simile, a comparison, a detail, or a member of a list, like this list from 1858.

> Nobody knows this little Rose—
> It might a pilgrim be
> Did I not take it from the ways
> And lift it up to thee.
> Only a Bee will miss it—
> Only a Butterfly,
> Hastening from far journey—
> On its breast to lie—
> Only a Bird will wonder—
> Only a Breeze will sigh—
> Ah Little Rose—how easy
> For such as thee to die!

And when we sample other bird references, we come up with such questions and answers as—does the morning have "feathers like a bird"?, or if "Water, is taught by Thirst" and "Land—by the Oceans passed," then birds are taught "by Snow." Or if Eden is "Old fashioned, then Birds are antiquated fellows!" And "the only Ghost I ever saw . . . was soundless, like the Bird." And as an unnamed cat "sights a Bird," it "chuckles." Sometimes a bird is simply a bird doing birdy things: "A Bird sat careless on the fence— / One gossipped in the Lane / On silver matters charmed a Snake / Just winding round a Stone—." In the second version of an 1864 poem, the "Wind began to rock the Grass" and from there, for sixteen more lines, the wind destroys and maims the whole near countryside, though "the Birds put up the Bars to Nests," and apparently survived. And in a late poem, "Things are not what they are" when they are "as guileless as a Bird."

Birds figure in every phase, packet, and period of Dickinson's writing life. As a presence they are almost episodic in their appearance throughout the poems, as if they are essential to the ongoing project—which, like so many other familiars in her work, they seem to be. Birds are certainly used as comparatives, but they are also, at times, correlatives. Nature as a theater of operations, in fact, represents the majority symbolic character of Dickinson's imagination—much more than her sometimes domestic, household interiors. Second to birds in the winged hierarchy are the bees, and after the bees, the butterflies, though this is not to dismiss her affection for trees, various grasses, flowers, stones, the sky in all shapes and weathers, and the day at all schedules of the light, and so forth. All of these phenomena are generalized or specifically termed depending on the focus of the particular poem.

But of the active principles, rather than the more passive tropes of nature in stasis, the birds predominate. Indeed, in an 1862 poem, 1862 perhaps being the poet's best year, the concept of Being itself—as an ontological reality—is enacted as a bird, a bird gladly celebrated:

Of Being is a Bird
The likest to the Down
An Easy Breeze do put afloat
The General Heavens—upon—

It soars—and shifts—and whirls
And measures with the Clouds
In easy—even—dazzling pace—
No different the Birds—

Except a Wake of Music
Accompany their feet—
As did the Down emit a Tune—
For Ecstasy—of it

More than twenty of the two hundred and twenty poems that reference birds are poems dedicated solely to the birds' single symbolic selves. The most famous, of course, is "A Bird came down the Walk," written also in 1862. It's an unusual instance in that Dickinson herself enters this bird poem as a participant rather than simply an observer. She comes in late to offer the bird on the walk a crumb—"walk" being a pun here, since it covers both the pathway and the means of walking. Which is to say the poem glosses and plays with a bird walking as opposed to a bird flying; that is, this particular bird is a Dickinson bird at Dickinson's human ground level. Naturally the poem elevates at the end: the bird's feathers rowing "him Softer Home—," at which point the poem leaps to a comparative of how "Oars divide the Ocean" and to a shift of swimming butterflies. It's a delightful and typical Dickinson mixture-of-metaphor exercise, though it isn't, like the vast majority of her bird-referenced poems, one of her very poignantly great ones.

But there is an early and there is a late bird poem each of genuine stature. They both contain robins, Dickinson's favorite poetry bird—a bird incredibly common, and large enough to really see: a good singer, a better-weather harbinger, a walker, and a worm eater. The male American robin's reddish-orange breast is like a vest, a chesty signature; its song, which Peterson describes as "caroling," is easily heard and recognizable. Whitman, you'll recall, speaks of the thrush's caroling in his elegy for Lincoln; and Keats, in "To Autumn," ends the poem with a red-breast whistling "from a garden-croft." You'd be hard put, in the spring, to tell much difference between the robin's singing and the thrush's song. One thing for sure, a robin is a democrat, not an aristocrat, hence Dickinson's interest. And a robin is not a skylark or a nightingale. In an 1859 poem that begins, beautifully, "Bring me the sunset in a cup"—a perfect Dickinson line—the poet moves quickly to its detail of a robin: "Write me how many notes there be / In the new Robin's ecstasy / Among astonished boughs—." It's true that Dickinson doesn't isolate the bird as the poem's single trope, but she does imbed it in a chorus of instruction that will free the poet of the bird cage of "this little Alban House" and will "let me out some gala day / With implements to fly away / Passing Pomposity."

The late poem, which wholly defines the robin as an emblem, is wonderful in its purity and demanding transformation of the object. It's written just six years before her death in 1886:

The Robin is a Gabriel
In humble circumstances—
His Dress denotes him socially,
Of Transport's Working Classes—
He has the punctuality
Of the New England Farmer—
The same oblique integrity,
A Vista vastly warmer—
A small but sturdy Residence,
A self denying Household,
The Guests of Perspicacity
Are all that cross his Threshold—
As covert as a Fugitive,
Cajoling Consternation
By Ditties to the Enemy
And Sylvan Punctuation—

This is the robin of robins, with qualities, first, of a holy messenger, then of a sterling farmer, then of a thoughtful and discerning homeowner, then of a smart and secret "fugitive." It's a poem of affection and buoyancy, without any death-watch or quarrel with the status-quo. Yet it recycles roles Dickinson the house-body sees herself playing. Like so much of her work, it marks Dickinson as a symbolist, a poet completely committed to the evocation and conversion of the meta-object and the byplay of form and content. For Dickinson the *ur* and ultimate subject is almost always poetry itself—self-referential, a thing made, but a thing made of multiples. The complexity in Dickinson derives from the simultaneity of her imagination, the at-onceness of the possibilities that make up the textures, images, and insights in her writing.

Nature is for her a neighbor, just outside the door, a familiar immediate place filled with familiars. And this "natural" world enlarges or reduces according to the required scale of the landscapes within the poems. While for all the physicality Dickinson sees there, the material manifestations are masks for an invisible world, the way her birds are images of ideas with bodies. Dickinson's second favorite bird, after the robin, is the unlikely bobolink, a songbird one ornithological wag describes as wearing a dress suit backwards—that is, black below and white above. How right for Dickinson that she would choose both the most common of birds and the most unusual looking and sounding: a robin, of course; but also a bird bobo-linked in its color in reverse, and with a gold crown to boot. And how right, too, that she would dote on birds that cover her bets, since the robin loves the ground, the worm, the walk, and the bobolink sings in flight and dwells among the tree distances. Then there's a third choice of lyric bird—the poet herself as a flyer. In one of her very last poems, she is afflicted by a snake-like worm in winter in her bedroom to which she responds by flying away to a sort of safety—to "Towns on from mine." Her escape, she says, was a dream.

It takes no Freud to realize the sexual metaphor implicit in the dream of flying, especially as the speaker seems both attracted to yet needs to escape the worm, the snake, and what she finally terms "Propitiation's claw," which is a typical Dickinson oxymoron, since to propitiate is to conciliate, to agree to, to accept, to reconcile—all of this willingness attached to a claw, an apparently dangerous sort of instrument. The stanza in which this image appears, in a thirty-nine line poem, runs like this, within the context of "my Room":

I shrank—"How fair you are"!
Propitiation's claw—
"Afraid," he hissed
"Of me"?
"No cordiality"—
He fathomed me—
Then to a Rhythm *Slim*
Secreted in his Form
As Patterns swim

Projected him.
That time I flew
Both eyes his way
Lest he pursue
Nor ever ceased to run
Till in a distant Town
Towns on from mine
I set me down
This was a dream.

Dickinson's response to her fantasy encounter with the "pink, lank and warm" worm is to become more than a bird but a bird-like thing that, instead of attacking, takes wing, flies away, only at last to "set me down," far, far from where she started. As far, in fact, as Eve, in the original Garden, in Book V of *Paradise Lost*, when the first woman is tempted by her "quick'n'd appetite…and "Could not but taste" the apple. "Forthwith up to the Clouds / With him I flew, and underneath beheld / The Earth outstretched immense." The difference between Dickinson and Eve, of course, is that Dickinson remains earthbound, flying to a distant place, while Eve is ascending—at least she thinks so—with her tempter.

Rowing in Eden

Ann Townsend

The only commandment I ever obeyed — 'Consider the Lilies.'
(L904)

On my desk an oiled stone that rests to serve as a reminder of its own heft and weight, and of the wall I am slowly building outside. Also on my desk: a grafting knife, a scattering of wooden plant markers, a half-empty bottle of ink, a book. The book is open to this poem, its initial lines:

A Pang is more conspicuous in Spring
In contrast with the things that sing
Not Birds entirely—but Minds—
And Winds—Minute Effulgencies
When what they sung for is undone
(F 1530)

In Emily Dickinson's poetry, the mind and the garden are one. The pain felt most clearly in spring attains its level of clarity because the spring garden is so beautiful, both visually and sonically, and is experienced so vividly as part of the mind's own landscape. In her poetry, the fertility of both mind and garden are dependent upon the safety of enclosure, upon walled and firm boundaries, and upon an essential privacy. The garden is a space in which to meditate, to create, to seek refuge. And, paradoxically, the garden's limitations also liberate.

A privileged space, a habitation the outside world cannot access: as she herself grew more reclusive, Dickinson arranged and shaped her landscape to reflect her vision of the world. Solitary, but never alone, she enfolded both her flowers and her poems into the epistles that made up her wide correspondence. These, in their way, served as her emissaries to the outside world: "Between My Country—and the Others— / There is a Sea— / But Flowers—negotiate between us— / As Ministry." (F 829)

The word paradise comes to us from Old Persian: *pairi* (around), and *diz* (to build a wall). In its original sense, a paradise was an enclosed garden. Emily Dickinson's poems and letters make frequent, nearly obsessive, reference to plants. Trace her use of the words "paradise" and "Eden," and you will find that Dickinson casts the garden as a manifestation of the human mind and soul. As a flower is to the garden, so is a poem to the mind, what Dickinson called "that garden unseen."

One: In 1855, Edward Dickinson constructed a small greenhouse for his daughter, attaching the structure to the southeast corner of the family home. The greenhouse's glassed-in microclimate allowed Emily Dickinson to cultivate the tropical plants she loved and granted her a small slice of summer during the prolonged New England winter. Her greenhouse was erected during the years when the production of plate glass, once a scarce and expensive commodity, was becoming more common. Before 1845, the high price of glass prohibited its large-scale use, but by mid-century glass-making techniques had advanced, and greenhouse manufacturers were soon selling and building relatively affordable glasshouses across the United States. The availability of economically priced greenhouse glass allowed nurseries and home gardeners alike to raise tender annual species and tropical plants from around the world.

Two: In his long narrative poem, published just one year before the 1855 construction of the Dickinson greenhouse, Coventry Patmore's "The Angel in the House" outlined the proper location of middle- and upper-middle class Victorian women, settled and protected inside a domestic landscape. The poem asserted that a woman's proper place is in the household, as mother, helpmeet, and steady inspiration for those around her: "Her disposition is devout, / Her countenance angelical; / The best things that the best believe / Are in her face so kindly writ / The faithless, seeing her, conceive / Not only heaven, but hope of it."

Patmore's position was itself the logical extension of a much older trope, in both art and literature, which depicted women securely ensconced at the center of a walled, enclosed garden. Medieval and renaissance *hortus conclusus* were living embodiments of the bridegroom's words in the *Song of Solomon* ("My sister, my bride, is a garden close-locked, a fountain sealed."). A *hortus conclusus* valorized the Christian model of chastity and was emblematic of the Virgin Mary's enclosed virginity. Pure and chaste, a desirable yet unattainable woman waits at the center of this garden.

Three: In 1887, the year after Emily Dickinson died, J. Atkinson Grimshaw painted what came to be seen as one of the quintessential paintings of the Victorian age. *The Rector's Garden: Queen of the Lilies* depicts a young woman who stands passively waiting in a walled garden. Stephen Kern describes it this way in *The Culture of Love: Victorians to Moderns:*

> in a [tightly] laced white dress [she] grasps a stalk of virginal white lilies. She is one more flower waiting to be picked. At the center of the garden is a ring of passionate red flowers. . . [that act as an emblem of] her own protected sexuality. . . . The garden's massive wall is covered with ivy—a long-growing, tenacious, and tangled protective cover. Her passive orientation to the future is [suggested by the presence of a tiny]. . . door in the wall. . . the door's small size, the surrounding ivy, and its remoteness from her reduce the odds of any man finding it or her.

Like the Angel in Patmore's poem, the ideal woman depicted here embodies piety, purity, obedience, a domestic ideal. A paper doll meant to define and inspire, she enjoys no particular voice of her own.

These three pieces of a Victorian landscape—the glass and iron greenhouse, Patmore's "The Angel in the House," Grimshaw's painting—offer the metaphors of womanhood that Dickinson lived with and was subject to. Each, in its way, suggests just how limited those domestic walls could be, just how small the doors and windows that seem to lead nowhere.

But in Dickinson's radical domesticity, walls provide shape for the wildness within; windows and doors contextualize the question

Dickinson asks in her 1878 letter to Judge Otis Phillips Lord: "Don't you know that 'No' is the wildest word we consign to Language?" (L562) For Dickinson, the enclosed garden provides shape and shelter for one who does not otherwise fit the dominant milieu, either socially or intellectually. An incubator for innovation, the garden allows for freedom from scrutiny and judgment.

For much of my adult life I have lived in intentional proximity to plants and trees; as the resident farmer at my own small Bittersweet Farm, I hybridize daylilies and iris, and cultivate tropical begonias and ferns on these ten acres. Each year between April and November I spend between six and nine hours a day working to tend and conserve the land whose every inch I love. I manage an orchard, a greenhouse, an enclosed garden, a pond, pasture, ravine, creek, woodland, and all of the creatures that feed and live and die in this place. This spring I will see the initial flowering of hundreds of seedling daylilies and iris, my own genetic crosses. In my greenhouse, I propagate tropical plants all winter long, most particularly those late Victorian favorites, the Rex and rhizomatous begonias that grew, perhaps, in Emily Dickinson's own conservatory.

I quite intentionally and happily live a private life. In this bounded and self-contained world, knowledge stems from intimate observation, from the daily round of sunrise and sunset, from patterns of rain and heat, from the minute changes in the land that can only be seen from close up, through long and sustained attention. It is an intensely physical life. The literary and environmental critic Angus Fletcher would call what I am describing "diurnal knowledge":

> knowledge of waking and not waking . . . of temporal change, which requires looking at natural phenomena with precision, so precisely indeed. . . that even delicate temporal shifts are made visible. . . . [Looking this way makes a place in poetry for] fragmentary, momentary, and seemingly inchoate experiences. . . .[D]iurnal knowledge is connected to the most basic human needs – living, breathing, sexuality, health, sickness. . . . It is above all seasonal knowledge. . . .

Dickinson locates her paradoxical freedom directly inside the boundaries of her garden; in its powerful presence she finds both a source for poetry, and a living, changing emblem for the life of the mind. Such deep engagement impels her to measure her own writing against the greater language of the natural world.

"My business is circumference," Emily Dickinson reminds her correspondent, Thomas Wentworth Higginson. Circumference for Dickinson is to be found in the contours and methods she uses, the patterns of repetition and parallel structures she relies upon: these reinforce Dickinson's allegiance to marking out distinct margins. Her strongly parallel sentences, her affinity for creating syllogistic arguments, and even the regularity of Dickinson's preferred hymn meter contain what Gaston Bachelard describes as a "felicitous space." These boundaries provide not only useful structure, but also paradoxically give the freedom that is inherent in individual privacy to do the imaginative work.

In "New feet within my garden go—" the poem's subject is spring's awakening, but the argument, guided by the parallel structure of the two stanzas and by the neat common meter, suggests that the shape of the poem and the structure of the garden move as one:

New feet within my garden go—
New fingers stir the sod—
A Troubadour upon the Elm
Betrays the solitude.

New Children play upon the green—
New Weary sleep below—
And still the pensive Spring returns—
And still the punctual snow!
(F 79)

The poem's structure embodies its own spatial metaphor: the poem's two stanzas balance rhetorically matched couplets, the first two lines of each stanza focusing on the "new" and the second two lines of each stanza moving outward to larger subjects of song and cyclical time. The poem's spatial sensibility creates a kind of garden grid or architecture, neat rows inside a strongly bounded frame. The common meter of the poem suggests that "feet" might as easily refer to poetic feet as to figures walking. The closing lines tell us that the seasons themselves follow their own means by their own measure.

Orson Welles claimed that "the enemy of art is the absence of limitations." Dickinson's unflinching poems have become touchstones for me as my farm has grown and prospered, as I myself have written and thrived in my own complex solitude. This week I watch the new season unfolding: the tree line's understory of young beech trees, then the pines and oaks, then the deep background of sycamores rising from the base of the ravine, some still bearing last year's leaves even as the understory takes on spring's green haze. Outside, I stop to dig three volunteer maples from the raspberry bed. I heel them in, into a corner of the compost bed, where they will stay until I'm ready to plant them in the woods. With my machete, I hack at the weeds and underbrush until I'm out of breath. It doesn't take long to be out of breath.

Each time I lose my breath, I am reminded that my immune system, which ought to produce antibodies in the presence of germs or disease, doesn't work that way for me. Instead, my immune system produces autoantibodies, which attack the organs of the body itself. This is what systemic lupus looks like. The lungs, the heart, the system of connective tissues break down under this insurgence.

So it is useful to remember that Emerson views gardening as a clarifying activity, one that provides a vantage point from which to see and comprehend. In his essay "Spiritual Laws," he suggests that when one is most truly him or herself, the world opens up beyond our imaginings. Each of us, he says,

> has his own vocation. The talent is the call. There is one

> direction in which all space is open to him. He has faculties silently inviting him thither to endless exertion. He is like a ship in a river; he runs against obstructions on every side but one; on that side all obstruction is taken away, and he sweeps serenely over a deepening channel into an infinite sea.

Dickinson relies upon the shapely confluence of inner and outer world, its unfolding, and what it reveals:

> There is a solitude of space
> A solitude of sea
> A solitude of death, but these
> Society shall be
> Compared with that profounder site
> That polar privacy
> A soul admitted to itself—
> Finite infinity.
> (J 1695)

The solitude of space, of sea, of death, is no match for the most severe solitude of all, that of self confronting self. A stable base (the finite) is dizzily lassoed to a kind of vertigo (infinity). So "Finite infinity" contains its own contradiction and reinforces the contrast between solitude as isolation and solitude as connection.

Emily Dickinson's poems do not live apart from the world; they *are* the world. Not innocent, not mild, not complicit in the becalmed lassitude and perfection of *The Rector's Garden*, but diurnal, passionate. The symmetry of Dickinson's poems lies in the way they connect knowledge both large and minute, in the way she seeks out correspondences between the natural world and the human world, and shows us a path, a way of thinking through a problem by analogy and representation. To be Emily Dickinson, alone with her intelligence and her imagination, is to be a hive filled with honey, to contain worlds wild with possibility, unchaste, alive, and most vivid in the present tense, which is, of course, all we have.

Hours

Carl Phillips

Familiarity is one way to think about what makes a home—a dailiness punctuated by routines that give a certain reliability to existence, or at least a perceived reliability. Routines are a way of parceling out time, and it's this human impulse toward measurement, quantification, mapping, that I want to consider here. Dickinson acknowledges a uselessness and/or irrelevance to this impulse to quantify abstraction, or to treat abstraction quantitatively, in a poem, for example, like 863 (Johnson), where she points out that estrangement is governed by something measureless:

> That Distance was between Us
> That is not of Mile or Main—
> The Will it is that situates—
> Equator—never can

And yet, over and over, Dickinson returns to the subject not just of time in general, but of specific months and seasons. Which is to say, she also acknowledges that, because our passing through time means being constantly vulnerable to the unpredictable, there's an unavoidable desire for something to correct for what she calls "a bland uncertainty." As she says in 1656, which tellingly begins by concretizing Time:

> Down Time's quaint stream
> Without an oar
> We are enforced to sail
> Our Port a secret
> Our Perchance a Gale
> What Skipper would
> Incur the Risk

What Buccaneer would ride
Without a surety from the Wind
Or schedule of the Tide—

Dickinson's frequent return to the months and seasons is an enactment, I think, of this desire for "surety" or "schedule," in the form of measurable time—and yet her descriptions often lead to a return to uncertainty, to liminality, as in 1404:

March is the Month of Expectation.
The things we do not know—
The Persons of prognostication
Are coming now—
We try to show becoming firmness—
But pompous Joy
Betrays us, as his first Betrothal
Betrays a Boy.

As I understand it, the uncertainty that characterizes expectation isn't initially being cast in a negative light. It's more that expectation makes us giddy with what good thing might be ahead for us. But the problem with expectation is that it leads to an immediate joy that blinds us to the other possibility, that of sorrow—a reminder, then, that expectation is characterized by uncertainty, the very uncertainty that we distract ourselves from by naming the months, ordering them, and thinking the resulting pattern makes us safe, when, as Dickinson says, "every way we fly / We are molested equally / By immortality" (1646).

In 1271, there's a desire to ground the abstraction of time in the concrete, but the poem ends up returning, as if inevitably, *to* abstraction:

September's Bacchalaureate
A combination is
Of Crickets—Crows—and Retrospects
And a dissembling Breeze

That hints without assuming—
An innuendo sear
That makes the Heart put up its Fun
And turn Philosopher.

Of course, in arriving at philosophy, we're in that field devoted to thinking about how to understand those most abstract concepts: knowing, behaving, existing. To my mind, philosophy is itself a field of trying to measure, or at least to solve for, human existence, not least of which is the fact of mortality, or more specifically, our consciousness of mortality. And I think mortality is ultimately always hovering behind Dickinson's concern with seasons, months, hours. Sometimes this is handled subtly, as in 1250:

White as an Indian Pipe
Red as a Cardinal Flower
Fabulous as a Moon at Noon
February Hour—

But you can see that the first two comparisons are to something fleeting, insofar as they are both flowers; not only that, but the Indian Pipe in particular is also known as "ghost flower" or "corpse flower," because it has no chlorophyll, is pale white, and lives entirely underground except when flowering. Meanwhile, a moon at noon is transient, and look how that final line implies a temporal diminuendo: February, an entire month, reducible to an hour, the dissolution of the nothingness that follows that final dash. And on the other hand, Dickinson can be quite overt in her association of the time with mortality, as in 656, where she describes Autumn in terms of the body as it bleeds away:

The name—of it—is "Autumn"—
The hue—of it—is Blood—
An Artery—upon the Hill—
A Vein—along the Road—

Great Globules—in the Alleys—
And Oh, the Shower of Stain—
When Winds—upset the Basin—
And spill the Scarlet Rain—

It sprinkles Bonnets—far below—
It gathers ruddy Pools—
Then—eddies like a Rose—away—
Upon Vermilion Wheels—

Note how, even in the last stanza, where she leaves the corporal metaphor behind, there's still the notion of mortality, of fleetingness, given the rose that must die, but also how the rose gets transformed into a carriage, something wheeled at least, caught departing.

The conundrum of time and the marking of it is that it becomes a constant reminder of our own limited time, compared to a forever that exists—what, outside us? Here's 1422:

Summer has two Beginnings—
Beginning once in June—
Beginning in October
Affectingly again—

Without, perhaps, the Riot
But graphicker for Grace—
As finer is a going
Than a remaining Face—

Departing then – forever—
Forever—until May—
Forever is deciduous—
Except to those who die—

Or is it that forever is what happens when the world is stripped of our quantifying systems, as Dickinson suggests in 624?

Forever—is composed of Nows—
'Tis not a different time—
Except for Infiniteness—
And latitude of Home—

From this—experienced Here—
Remove the Dates—to These—
Let Months dissolve in further Months—
And Years—exhale in years—

Without Debate—or Pause—
Or Celebrated Days—
No different Our Years would be
From Anno Domini's—

The closest we can get, maybe, to this kind of forever is to lie fixed in the now, between what has happened and what might. Is this what Dickinson means when she says "I dwell in Possibility" (657)? And yet, this possibility is the same as the uncertainty, the constant presence of risk as we pass down the stream of time—right?

How can forever be both deciduous and composed of Nows—an endless present? Here, Dickinson reminds me a bit of Augustine's concerns about time in his *Confessions,* where he suggests that there is only finally the present, and "the present considering the past is the memory, the present considering the present is immediate awareness, the present considering the future is expectations" [XIX.xx(26)]. It's Augustine who says that the Word of God is spoken, not in the realm of time, but "in the simultaneity of eternity. Otherwise time and change would already exist, and there would not be a true eternity and true immortality" [XI.vii(9)]. I'm not sure, but I have the feeling that Dickinson is touching somehow upon this idea in 1056, where time itself seems to have disappeared, or to be in abeyance, but an abeyance that seems to be eternal, since it depends upon seeming impossibilities:

There is a Zone whose even Years
No Solstice interrupt—

Whose Sun constructs perpetual Noon
Whose perfect Seasons wait—

Whose Summer set in Summer, till
The Centuries of June
And Centuries of August cease
And Consciousness—is Noon.

I believe her. Or at least I want to—a kind of faith.
But where *is* this place?

Thresholds

David Baker

Emily Dickinson entered into this world on December 10, 1830, in Amherst, Massachusetts, and died in the same town, in the family homestead, "quite suddenly" as her friend Clara Newman Turner wrote on May 15, 1886. She was fifty-five years old. Her doctor listed the cause as Bright's disease (what we now call nephritis or kidney failure) and its duration as two and a half years. Already Clara Newman Turner's "quite suddenly" is one of countless misrepresentations we find about Emily Dickinson. In 1885, Dickinson wrote that she saw "a great darkness coming" and fainted while baking in the kitchen. On November 30, 1885, her weakness was so worrying that her brother, Austin, canceled a trip to Boston. She spent the next months in bed. The last thing she wrote was that famous haiku-like note to the Norcross sisters: "Little Cousins, Called Back. Emily." Austin remembered in his diary that "the day was awful . . . she ceased to breathe that terrible breathing just before the whistle sounded for six."

Emily Dickinson never married. She was in love once, twice, maybe three times; it's hard to tell. There is so much legend. But she did indeed favor white for clothing. She was often accused of being shy—aloof, apart. "Best things dwell out of sight," she whispers. For years her privacy was directed at unfamiliar company, though by the end she hid from almost everyone but Austin and her sister Lavinia, or conversed from behind the cracked door of her threshold. She graduated from Amherst Academy in 1847. The following year brought the longest time she was ever away from home, when she attended Mount Holyoke Female Seminary. It was ten miles away. She stayed for ten months. And so, at the age of seventeen, Emily Dickinson came home and turned herself into a primary housekeeper, rarely leaving again. The farthest she got from Amherst came in the spring of 1855, when she, her mother, and her sister spent three weeks in Washington D.C., where her father served in Congress as a Massachusetts representative; they stopped on the way home in Philadelphia for two weeks of family visits.

It's hard not to abide by categories of gendered stereotypes when recounting her life. It is how she lived. Shira Wolosky deems that Dickinson's gendered norms are so extreme as to radicalize those norms: "Dickinson's is modesty with a vengeance, more explosive than obedient, more challenging than conforming." She was a decent cook; my students recently made her coconut cake from the recipe we have in her unmistakable slant of hand. She was a good seamstress. And she was a remarkable observer, a naturalist, a birder, and a deeply invested gardener. Her father, Edward, gifted her with a greenhouse, a "conservatory" they called it, in 1851. It faced east and south and adjoined the family dining room. Edward hoped to keep his daughter happy during the long winter months of the Northeast, when the death of a flower could bring her profoundest grief: "My acquaintance with the Irreparable," she wrote, "dates from the Death Bed of a young flower to which I was deeply attached." Judith Farr suggests that Edward felt gardening might be a more suitable pastime than poetry for a socially elevated young woman. But eventually the sober lawyer, the righteous Christian, found his daughter's gardening to be "disproportionate, irreligious," and tried to steer her toward her "one talent": baking.

We find her talent to be poetry. I find her the single most ferocious, terrifying, and intrepid lyric poet of our language—with Milton, Blake, maybe Berryman, maybe Plath, for the sheer proximity to chaos, devastation, psychic and physical rupture, obliteration. Yet she wrote about what was right there, at the window, out the door, in the trees or the sitting room of the big house on Main Street. She wrote a poetry of intimacy and intimate proximity.

She wrote and wrote—more than 1800 poems. Between 1858 and1866, she wrote at least a thousand of those poems. In a remarkably short period—namely during the years of the Civil War—she wrote more than eight hundred of those. I did the math. From April 12, 1862, and the firing on Ft. Sumter to April 9, 1865, and Lee's surrender at Appomattox, I count 1458 days.

Eight hundred poems. That cannot be a coincidence, though only three or four poems refer to the war in recognizable detail. Anxiety is a mighty powerful translator. Two hundred and twenty of these poems came during the incredible year of 1862, the year of her first crisis, her mysterious leap to radical intensity, morbidity, and greatness. Critics make of the crisis what they will: depression; a failed love affair; seasonal affective disorder; the onset of Bright's; melancholia; bipolar dysfunction; artistic imbalance. She herself saw little difference between such physical or metaphysical causes. She specifically resists such pat categorical explanations: "Twas Crisis—All the length had passed—- / That dull—benumbing time / There is in Fever or Event— / And now the Chance had come." Interestingly, 1862 was the year of another chance, one of her biggest personal risks. This is the year she first wrote to Thomas Wentworth Higginson—again in April, on the 15th, to be exact—to ask him "what is true," to find out if her "Verse is alive."

Dickinson saw only seven of her poems—unattributed—published in periodicals. "Publication is the Auction of the mind of man," she reminds. Then again, she published much of her work herself. She wrote out final drafts of her poems in ink on fine paper, ordered specially. She used all of a page. The pages came pre-folded once; she arranged them into groups, from eleven to twenty poems—chronological perhaps, thematic, who knows—stacked them carefully, punched two holes in them, and tied them with good string. These packets, these fascicles, were her books. There were ultimately forty of them. "This is my letter to the World / That never wrote to Me," indeed. And when she died, Mabel Loomis Todd took more than six hundred and sixty-five of those poems and stuck them in a camphorwood chest and closed the lid.

"The Soul selects her own Society— / Then—shuts the Door."

Dickinson's enforced isolation provides two things for her: stability and alternity. Yet the door to Dickinson's imagination was open to what was near, the daily, the nigh, and the known. Tangible, present objects populate her poetry with sparkling clarity. Who can do an image like Dickinson? "Split the Lark—and you'll find the Music— / Bulb after Bulb, in Silver rolled." "Shame is the shawl of

Pink / In which we wrap the Soul / To keep it from infesting eyes." Her phenomena, her things—be they concrete or abstract, physical or metaphysical—may be wildly idiosyncratic but they are also entirely recognizable. That's what I mean by alternity. "Through the Dark Sod—as Education— / The Lily passes sure / Feels her white foot—no Trepidation— / Her faith—no fear." She's as lyrical as Whitman. "If you were coming in the Fall, / I'd brush the Summer by / With half a smile, and half a spurn, / As Housewives do, a fly. // If I could see you in a year, / I'd wind the months in balls— / And put them each in separate Drawers, / For fear the numbers fuse." She can whittle an aphorism like Emerson or Franklin. "It was not Death, for I stood up, / And all the Dead, lie down." "Dreams—are well—but Waking's better." This is my favorite: "To fill a Gap / Insert the Thing that caused it . . . / You cannot solder an Abyss / With Air."

Flowers and birds, gates and grasses, a gentlemanly god in a top hat, a "visitor in Marl," fathers and snakes, platters, a "small Leech" and a "Dying Tiger," snowflakes, horses, church organs: tangible objects populate Dickinson's very particularizing poetry, mixing with erotic, holy, naturalistic, and familial newness. For someone so isolated, agoraphobic, Dickinson's poetry is tremendously busy, abuzz; it is as social as a nation. George Steiner writes that "Dickinson knew that her solitude was crowded with presences." She confirms: "Alone I cannot be— / For Hosts do visit me— / Recordless Company—Who baffle key." Just as Shira Wolosky finds the paradox of Dickinson's gendered norms to be "radicalized" into "explosive" obedience, I want to identify another central paradox: that, as Steiner puts it, "Dickinson makes of her isolation the fuel, the validation of an illumined strangeness."

I want to press on that illumined strangeness as I lead to a couple of personal claims. It's not just the fabulous clarity of her images, her material and immaterial substances that vivify Dickinson's poetry with such force. Nor is it just the rhetorical certitude with which she authorizes her judgments and observations, for indeed she is powerful in her claims ("Out of sight? What of that? / See the Bird—reach it! / Curve by Curve—Sweep by Sweep— / Round the Steep

Air— / Danger! What is that to Her? / Better 'tis to fail—there— / Than debate—here."). But she arranges her population so carefully, into so highly socialized an order of relationships, and invests that order with such meaningful purpose, that it's fair to say she writes as a latter-day allegorist. I can think only of Blake as a kindred lyric allegorist in all the 19th century. Each of her recurring tropes—birds and the church, herbs and heredity—brings a body of knowledge, a set of allusions, and a doctrinal history, which Dickinson knew precisely, and used. She knew the tenets and testaments of her father's church, just as she knew the hermit thrush and bobolink both build their nests on the ground, even when there's available higher vegetation. She devoured the floral dictionaries of her day, where each flower and herb is assigned specific connotations, history, and uses, so her poetry's constant horticultural associations are exact and shared. These things consolidate her participation in the culture of the day.

To read Dickinson is to read a poetry with a moral scheme equal in depth, if not in consistency, to Dante's. Her landscapes, even in miniature, are charged with meaning in themselves but also beyond themselves; they are haunted with spirits like a Charles Burchfield canvas, eyes and wings and shadows over shadows; they are layered and tiered with intention and intimations of immortality: "Presentiment—is that long Shadow—on the Lawn— / Indicative that Suns go down." These poems are not, decidedly, Christian. Dickinson understood her own blasphemy as clear as a bell; she nurtured it. But her poems are deeply faithful, Romantic if not conventionally Calvinist: "Some keep the Sabbath going to Church— / I keep it, staying at Home— / With a Bobolink for a Chorister— / And an Orchard, for a Dome." In fact, her morality, her ultimate faith and investment, is an esthetic's morality, much as Keats's or Stevens's. She concludes the impeccable argument of this poem with a typical zinger: "So instead of getting to Heaven, at last— / I'm going, all along."

Emily Dickinson's private lyric world is full of presences. But for all the presences mentioned in this symposium, there's one more I find central to understanding her imagination and her cosmology.

One more intimacy, one more intimate proximity, and that is Capital D, Death. "Because I could not stop for Death— / He kindly stopped for me." Like the blue-fringed gentian, like the "executive" jay coming down the walk, death is a presence near at hand, and knocking. And its presence illuminates the other presences like no other, not even God. "Death," she writes, "sets a Thing significant."

Odysseus journeys to the ends of the earth, and beneath it, to confront and confound the demons of the dead. Dante travels down circle by circle into the Inferno of the damned. In Dickinson's day, Melville sails the seas to face that oceanic abyss, the consuming, terrifying, whitening, outstretching obliteration of identity. The great writers before her situate death at a distance, a great distance—whether up or down or way out there—and measure the merit of their task in part by the length of their odyssey to and from the world of the dead.

Dickinson's robin is just there, on a limb at the window. And death, too, is just as near and neighborly: "I died for Beauty—but was scarce / Adjusted in the Tomb / When One who died for Truth, was lain / In an adjoining room." This is her "strange negative space," as Maureen McLane puts it, her Keatsian "posthumous condition" that can generate "an uncanny aliveness in voice and mind." When she feels that famous funeral in her brain, she inhabits both congregation and coffin in the little church that is her bodily residence, home. And when the "Plank in Reason" breaks, she falls through this world into other worlds, each atop the other, as tiered and as haunted as all her other social relationships. Terror is the second dominant feature of Dickinson's poetry, counterpoint to the joyful natural pleasure she so often finds. But terror is not only the fact of death; it's the nearness at hand, the neighborly, mannerly, at-first gentlemanly omnipresence that is, ultimately, obliterating and consuming.

Helen Vendler finds this to be the defining feature of Dickinson's designs, the destination of her rhetoric; or better, the cause of the primary rupture of that rhetoric. Death, the rupturer, the eraser, "breaks the sequence or seriality" so important to Dickinson's lyricism. It perhaps explains the powerful appropriateness of those ever-present dashes, the little rip in syntax, the gap, the break, the gasp-for-breath. Formally the dashes enact—they make material—that very "Capacity to terminate," as Dickinson writes. "The great crisis in Dickinson's work arrives when her instinctive practice of serial . . . chromate advance encounters unavoidable fissure, fracture, rupture, or abyss," says Vendler. Dickinson put it better: "I felt a Cleaving in my Mind." Her frequent sequencing—and then, and then, and then—is disrupted by the finality of the end-point death. "First—Chill—then Stupor—then the letting go." After which utterance there is no more to say, because there is no word to say it, only the horses' heads pointing *toward* eternity: snow, white paper, "White Sustenance," the silence beyond the place where the meanings are.

Here is my final point and the last paradox I want to propose. I have gone to some lengths to show that Dickinson's treatment of daily detail is as close to allegory as we are likely to get in the 19th century. She highly stylizes the flowers and birds, the gods and stones and dimples and cordial women, and sets them into a shared, socialized order of relationships, where meaning resides atop meaning and artistic imagination is the supreme fiction. But with death, in her hundreds of treatments of death, Dickinson abandons allegory for the real. There are no translations of death, no dense mythologies for death, as there are no real words for it, only breakage, fissure, gap, rupture. Where there are no words, there is no fancy nor figure and can be no meaning: "The Silence condescended— / Creation stopped—for Me— / But awed beyond my errand— / I worshipped—did not 'pray.'" She cannot pray for there are no words when we are "awed beyond" our errand.

For me, Dickinson's magic is that she takes us closer to that rupture than any other lyric poet. Or maybe, with Keats and Whitman she stands as our most significant pre-post-modernist in this regard. Erasure, absence, the disenfigured gap, rhetorical incompatibility, the unresolved thing, the always already ever-beyond-our-reach: We think we have invented that in our belated state? Think again. Emily Dickinson has been there. Like Whitman, who knows but she is looking at us right now. That second-story window on Main Street in Amherst, Massachusetts, has one beguiling view.

Wallace Stevens

THE MIND AT THE END OF THE PALM

Feeling Thinking

David Baker

"We think by feeling," writes Roethke in a beautiful poem, and then adds with a lyric shrug, "what is there to know?" Roethke articulates in "The Waking" a manner of late, purified, and some have said discredited Romanticism—more inspiration than intellect, more sense than sanity or reason. So he doesn't get lost in his unknowing, in a dark time, Roethke finds his way in and back out of the maze by means of form itself, following the step-by-step, syllable-by-syllable guidance of the villanelle. Otherwise, it might all look like, well, disaster.

Wallace Stevens is one of our supreme knowers, one of the profound thinkers of, and inside, the lyric poem. If Roethke thinks by feeling, then how does Stevens think? All that abstract longwinded highbrow stuff, that tink-a-tink and philosophy, what to do with all that?

Philosophy is my first point, or rather the relation of philosophy to the lyric utterance. One of the persisting characterizations of Stevens and his poems—and it seems everyone has written on Stevens—is that he is a philosophical poet, that particular kind of abstractive thinker. Even a quick amble through recent Stevens criticism will show the commentators as likely to position Stevens alongside philosophers as alongside poets. Of course, there's Burke and Kermode, James and Santayana and Locke; but Stevens and Derrida, Gombrich, Adorno, Bachelard, Blanchot, Wittgenstein, Lacan, Pater, Levinas, Hegel, Schlegel, Kant. Entire books appear about Stevens and the philosophical: *The Never-Resting Mind*, *The Act of the Mind*, *Stevens's Poetry of Thought*, and *A Cure of the Mind*. This last title derives from one of those delicious adages from Stevens's own "Adagia," those great baffling clarities, those one- and two-sentence zingers of which Americans are so fond. Poetry, he says, is a cure of the mind. He also says there is no wing like meaning. Poetry is a health, he says; but then, poetry must be irrational. He says it is the spirit, but also it is a meteor, it is money, it is a café, it is a daily necessity for "getting things right." Even while, as he says, "[i]n the end the truth does not matter." If philosophy is a love of truthful thinking, then is he actually an anti-philosopher?

At some point Stevens says almost everything and includes almost everything. And in the case of criticism, his work can be made to fit, to prove, to substantiate, and to dramatize almost every stance toward Platonism, the Socratic method, but also pre-Socraticism as well as neo-Platonism, Romanticism, Realism, Metaphysics, Phenomenology, and more.

Wallace Stevens is one of the great lyric chameleons. Is he a philosopher?

I have my feelings about that question, but I'm also trained just enough in philosophy to know I'm not well trained in philosophy. So I asked three poetry friends, who by profession are philosophers: Who are the most important philosophical poets, and is Stevens one of them? What is philosophical poetry?

Troy Jollimore, with his specialty in "agent-relative morality," reports that "I have given this a lot of thought over the last few days [there's a philosopher playing with you] and have come up with very little." Pope perhaps, he says, as "he does sort of follow a train of argument rather as an analytic philosopher would." But even here, says Jollimore, "the form overwhelms the inquiry."

Kascha Semonovich—trained in continental philosophy, where people are "more accommodating to 'poetic' philosophy"—says "I personally don't think philosophy and poetry are terribly similar." She supposes Oppen as kind of philosophical, and moments of Hass or Graham, but makes a significant differentiation between sustained analysis and mere "philosophical moments": no system of philosophical position laid out; no sustained justification in the procedure; and "without justification you just have beliefs."

And John Koethe, with his work on Wittgenstein and on skepticism, makes a great distinction, using Stevens himself—and this seems crucial to me—between systematic thinking and "the movements of consciousness." He concurs with Helen Vendler that "the guiding impulse of Stevens's poetry is not an intellectual construction but rather a sense of dissatisfaction." I would add to this: a dissatisfaction in the very system of intellectual construction that defines both philosophy and the logical or reasonable rhetoric of legal argument out of which Stevens's very day-job derives.

So to the first question, how and when is lyric poetry philosophical? That is, when does it "do" philosophy? Almost never. Maybe some of Lucretius? A stretch or two of Milton, Wordsworth? Milosz? To be philosophy, a text should somehow, somewhere, sustain a specific type of investigation: analytic, reasonable, and progressive. It should enact a system of analysis, a procedure and what Semonovich calls "sustained justification in the procedure." And in its procedure, doesn't a philosophical text accumulate evidence and distill that evidence, summarizing with reason toward a kind of radical synthesis? It works toward a theory of things rather than toward a thing itself. And is that perhaps the opposite of the lyric's devotion to particularity or specificity; or, in Stevens's case, oddity and eccentricity, even abstract exceptionalism? Bart Eeckhout in "Stevens and Philosophy" determines that "when we try to situate Stevens's poetry within the most important philosophical traditions in Western history, we cannot but be struck by how relevant almost all of them are to his kind of thinking and writing—with one major exception: that of analytic philosophy." And he counts among analytic philosophers everyone from Plato and Aristotle to Derrida and beyond.

Let's say that Stevens is not a philosophical poet at all. Then what is he? We know he was educated at Harvard, took his law degree from New York Law School. Yet it appears he never took a single philosophy course. His contemporary T. S. Eliot wrote an entire doctoral thesis in philosophy, on F. H. Bradley, called *Knowledge and Experience*, a tract on metaphysics and practical activity. Yet even Eliot's poetry is less philosophical than narrative—as in "Prufrock"—or dramatic, as in *The Wasteland*. I'd like to propose three kinds of rhetorical paradigms in Stevens's poetry, none of them ultimately "doing" philosophy.

First here—and first in his poetic chronology—are those

crystalline Imagist poems. I refer to his early poems with their strange landscapes, their odd characters (pueriles, Polish aunts, inchling chieftains, dawdling wenches, simpering Byzantines with noisy tambourines) doing inexplicable things. These are still-life vignettes, portraits of surreal clarity, devoid of the "plain sense" of things. Or perhaps they indeed are enacting plain or obvious things—they're just making ice cream in the kitchen, after all, in "Emperor of Ice Cream," where that dead lady lies covered-up in the next bedroom—obvious things oddly said. "Out of my mind," he writes, "the golden ointment rained." Here it's not ideas but rather the irrational "golden ointment of imagination" that issues from his thinking. "I was the world in which I walked, and what I saw / Or heard or felt came not but from myself; / And there I found myself more truly and more strange."

Even in the strangeness of his Imagism, he seems inclined to suggest—and to parody—a kind of methodology. Not philosophy but the appearance of philosophical method. What is that famous blackbird poem if not a lyric version of the building of a case, by the evidentiary presence and process of examples? Exhibit A: "A man and a woman / Are one." Exhibit B: "A man and a woman and a blackbird / Are one." Skipping ahead: Exhibit G: "I know noble accents / And lucid, inescapable rhythms; / But I know, too, / That the blackbird is involved / In what I know." Ah, evidence *and* precedent. But what do we *know*? What *do* these shards and exactitudes prove, exactly? What is the thinking here, after Exhibit M and Q? He says in summary, as in syllogism: "It was evening all afternoon. / It was snowing / And it was going to snow. / [ergo] The blackbirds sat / In the cedar-limbs." So he presents not process but a pastiche of process: around and around, ultimately unable to see the whole picture but always aware of the omnipresence, like blunt fate, of that blackbird. Less omen than bird. Less thought than datum. Less meaning, less philosophy, than a tautology of the indecipherable, that darkly comic accompaniment.

As Stevens's work matures (and remember, he doesn't publish his first book, *Harmonium*, until he's 44), he pushes his logical-seeming method of making patterns into something more rhetorically sustained. I'll call this his second type of lyric: the speculative poem. This stands for Stevens at the rhetorical pole farthest from his Imagist work. Perhaps this is the type that comes closest to philosophy. When one speculates, one takes or aims at a stance, and goes purposefully in search of the end of that stance. This is Stevens as epistemologist. He shares with philosophers a questioning: what do we know, and how do we know what we know? He writes in *The Necessary Angel* that the poet seeks a power "to have such insights into reality as will make it possible for him to be sufficient as a poet in the very center of consciousness."

His great poem, "Esthetique du Mal," serves as a speculative example, a poem in which Stevens hopes to "communicate / The intelligence of his despair, express / What meditation never quite achieved." Here in the "unpeopled" aloneness of things, he "disposes the world in categories," wondering at the "knowledge of himself." "Which," he asks, "is more desperate in the moments when / The will demands that what he thinks be true?" Though he seems to build a careful case, in the end his very speculation creates "a third world without knowledge." "The extreme of logic" produces, by paradox, "illogic": "'I followed his argument / With the blank uneasiness which one might feel / In the presence of a logical lunatic." His supposed hero, the logical, is ultimately also the ultimate failure: "he would be the lunatic of one idea / In a world of ideas . . . He would not be aware of the clouds / Lighting the martyrs of logic with white fire. / His extreme of logic would be illogical." Gone in search of conclusion, what he finds is its baffling opposite. Among his other poems that suit this category—the speculative lyric—I might list "The Comedian as the Letter C," "Examination of the Hero in a Time of War," "Connoisseur of Chaos," "Description without Place," and "Things of August."

Finally, and in his finest poems, and the majority of his poems, Stevens exercises his favorite rhetorical method: not doing philosophy, but rather meditating on things and ideas. He notes some dissatisfaction with meditation, as in "Esthetique du Mal," citing his desire to "express what meditation never quite achieved." But to me, he is most truly a meditative poet. Let's say his Imagist poems hover, static, halted. And let's say that to speculate is to drive forward, with determination, a destination in mind. Then to meditate is to amble. Meditation is an open-ended gambit to see less where one ends up than what one notices along the way. It is an amusement, a kind of Emersonian circle—observing, orbiting, musing and amused by "this vast ebb of a vast flow": Stevens as transparent eyeball, observing, as John Koethe calls it, "the movements of consciousness." Think of him walking home from work at Hartford Indemnity. In fact, Roger Gilbert treats this meditative aspect of Stevens with this same trope: the meditative "walk," not as a narrative subject, but rather its occasion, "the experience out of which the poem seems to arise and of which it is itself a part."

"An Ordinary Evening in New Haven" is one of Stevens's great poems and an example of the meditative lyric, composed in blank verse. Here is the category of Stevens's most frequent rhetoric. He is an "ephebe . . . solitary in his walk"; "a strong mind in a weak neighborhood"; seeking neither the knowledge of the "priest nor proctor," seeking in fact only a transcript of "the never-ending meditation." The thirty-one sections of this magnificent poem come to closure not when his analytic method reaches deduction or conclusion, but rather when the walker simply arrives, having trod "the metaphysical streets of the physical town." "We keep coming back and coming back to the real." A whirl of amusements—from the theological to the earthy, the personal to the all—the poem in meditation mediates "the philosopher's search / For an interior made exterior / And the poet's search for the same exterior made / interior." It's as much music as method, and more amusement than analysis. He wants it all, thoughtful discovery but accident, too, comedic unreality: "If it should be true that reality exists / In the mind . . . it follows that / Real and unreal are two in one"; and that "Flickings from finikin to fine finikin" are as substantial as "a shade that traverses / A dust."

In this grand work we are listening to music in a mind freely playing, openly wondering, and aswirl. So that, so simply—as he writes in "Description without Place," with its plain purpose to transcribe "the way / Things look each day, each morning"—the imagination may be more alive "with its own seemings." This effect prompts Gilbert to conclude that "[the occasion of this poem] becomes a source of authentic vision, a way of seeing the world in its essential integrity while recognizing that it, like the walker, remains caught up in motion . . . [a] fluid process. [It] gives us a metaphysics of the walk, in which movement subsumes real and unreal, visible and invisible, poem and occasion."

Absolutely Stevens shares with philosophers a love of thinking and an abstractive bent. More important, he shares a fundamental epistemology: questioning what we know, and how we know it. He makes use of systems, procedures, and, at times, a methodology that seems like philosophy. But it is more truly a parody of philosophy: both a comedian's send-up and an agnostic's rebuff. Not analysis but meditation; not understanding but, as Gilbert puts it, a "kinetics of experience." *In Discourse on Thinking*, Heidegger gives us an exacting distinction: "Thinking may take one of two forms: calculative thinking, which is driven by the will, and meditative thinking, which enables and is enabled by an openness to the mystery of existence."

There it is. Roethke says, "I think by feeling." I propose that Stevens says, "I feel by thinking." That may be the closest I can come to an aesthetic theory of Stevens's poetry. He thinks, and in thinking—deeply, wildly, in ways systematic and unruly alike—his thinking enables his feeling. Thinking makes him nearly ecstatic.

Wallace Stevens and the Predicate of Substance

Linda Gregerson

"The poet," writes Sir Philip Sidney, "nothing affirmeth." And no poet ever conformed more religiously to this secular injunction than Wallace Stevens. Critics have noted for decades his predilection for the subjunctive and interrogative moods, the floating infinitives and participial phrases, the dizzying array of "ifs" and "as ifs," the elaborated syntactical dependencies designed to baffle the most assiduous reader. The poet nothing affirmeth and therefore never lies. And yet, one feels the need for something more.

In a letter from August 1942, Stevens wrote to Harvey Breit about a visit he had just made to the Reformed Protestant Dutch Church in Kingston, New York, "one of the most beautiful churches that I know of," he wrote, "improved by the fact that it has a pleasant janitor with a red nose." Stevens was especially impressed when the janitor supplied him with a little pamphlet written by one of the church's most distinguished parishioners, one Justice Gilbert Hasbrouck, and goes so far as to transcribe its opening lines, which are as follows:

> Indeed when Spinoza's great logic went searching for God it found Him in a predicate of substance . . .

Stevens comments: "Now, if a lawyer as eminent as Judge Hasbrouck went to church because it made it possible for him to touch, to see, etc., the very predicate of substance, do you think he was anything except a poet?"

In the eighth canto of "The Auroras of Autumn," published some six years later by John Crowe Ransom in *The Kenyon Review*, Stevens seems to recall that little pamphlet in the Reformed Dutch Church:

There may be always a time of innocence.
There is never a place. Or if there is no time,
If it is not a thing of time, nor of place,

Existing in the idea of it, alone,
In the sense against calamity, it is not
Less real. For the oldest and coldest philosopher,

There is or may be a time of innocence
As pure principle. Its nature is its end,
That it should be, and yet not be, a thing

That pinches the pity of the pitiful man,
Like a book at evening beautiful but untrue,
Like a book on rising beautiful and true.

It is like a thing of ether that exists
Almost a predicate.

I find innocence to be a rather shocking invocation in a poem so saturated with epistemological doubt—this is its first appearance in the poem, but it will recur obsessively in this and the following canto, seven times altogether. That Stevens, being Stevens, accorded to the concept no simple powers of anchoring stability we may tend to assume, and this assumption is buttressed by an earlier appearance of the term in "Esthetique du Mal": "That he might suffer or that / He might die was the innocence of living, if life / Itself was innocent." A very big if, for Wallace Stevens. But he recognized a structural necessity for the concept—"not less real"—and in "Auroras of Autumn," it is oppositionally entangled with the figure of the serpent, who begins as a constellation in the Northern sky, one easiest to discern in the autumn of the year, unless it is occluded by the gaudier Aurora Borealis, also at the height of visibility, in Hartford, in the autumn months. Milton describes the serpent on the grassy herb—just before it is entered by the spirit of Satan—as "not nocent yet." Nocent: present participle of nocēre, to hurt or injure. Thus, in the common understanding of the matter, to be innocent is to be harmless, not yet capable of doing harm. But also, as the myth makes clear, innocence is a state of not-yet-being-harmed oneself, since the capacity for evil is itself a kind of suffered harm, albeit, in the myth, a self-inflicted suffering.

The myths we inherit pass through many hands before they come to us, and are forever altered when those hands are capable ones: I'm convinced that Stevens had Milton in mind when he composed this poem. The forbidding father "leaps from heaven to heaven more rapidly / Than bad angels leap from heaven to hell in flames." "The Auroras of Autumn" is a northern imaginary, fixated upon the "Arctic effulgence" of the northern sky: in *Paradise Lost*, Satan gathers his rebellious angels in the regions of the North. Stevens's serpent begins as a constellation, a "body flashing without the skin" amidst the auroras (the false dawns of a late season) that manifest a thing we might find impossibly hypothetical (the magnetic fields of the earth) were it not for the evidence of our senses. The serpent becomes a governing principle: "master of the maze / Of body and air and forms and images, / Relentlessly in possession of happiness." Happiness, which we only know because of his powers to take it away. "This is his poison," writes Stevens, "that we should disbelieve / Even that."

Belief, then, is innocence—the not yet poisoned state. But upon what ground to plant it?

> It is like a thing of ether that exists
> Almost as a predicate.

The predicate of substance. Substance: the *the*, as Stevens so eloquently puts it in "The Man on the Dump." Grammatically, the predicate is one of two main constituents of a sentence or clause: the verb, or action word, and all those objects and modifiers governed by the verb. So God (subject) returns to judge the quick and the dead (predicate all). In logic, the predicate is that part of a proposition that is affirmed or denied about the subject. So all men (subject) + are mortal (predicate). The subject would seem to come first. And yet predicate, in logic (prae [before] + dicāre [proclaim]), comes to have the force of that-which-came-before, the foundation upon which the subject is based. Substance manifests itself in motion only. So which comes first: the serpent or the egg from which it wriggles?

The serpent presides over the early cantos of "Auroras of Autumn," but innocence nearly banishes it from the figurative field:

> It is a thing of ether that exists
> Almost as predicate. But it exists,
> It exists, it is visible, it is, it is.
>
> So, then, these lights are not a spell of light,
> A saying out of a cloud, but innocence.
> And innocence of the earth and no false sign
>
> Or symbol of malice. That we partake thereof,
> Lie down like children in this holiness,
> As if, awake, we lay in the quiet of sleep,
>
> As if the innocent mother sang in the dark
> Of the room and on an accordion, half-heard,
> Created the time and place in which we breathed . . .

Innocence with the power to make a time and human breathing place is not, for Stevens, originary innocence. It is not—in Milton's fabulous formulation—mere excremental whiteness. It is innocence achieved, which assumes the power of predication. It is a castle in the air, precisely, as solid a foundation as the "round earth's imagined corners," which for John Donne are the solid sign of divinity's accommodation to the scale of the human mind.

The predicate of substance is an irreducible oxymoron, or perhaps it would be more accurate to call it an aporia: the predicate depends upon the substance, and the substance upon the predicate; each is metaphysical foundation for the other. The auroras of autumn—the light of early day in a late hour of a late year, the visible tracings of invisible forces—are an irreducible aporia. "Aporia," which George Puttenham calls "the Doubtful, . . . because oftentimes we will seeme to cast perils, and make doubt of things when by a plaine manner of speech we might affirme or deny him." What Puttenham took for a figure of rhetoric, recent semiotics and philosophy have taken for a foundational condition of language. Innocence is an aporetic configuration: the negation of a prior state (nocence) of which innocence can have no knowledge. Innocence, which can only be imagined, "almost as a predicate." But is. It is.

Perhaps the most striking aspect of Steven's autumnal poem, for me, at this season, is its recourse to the first person plural. There is a place for private memory: the formidable father, the mother's face. But the time and place that innocence engenders is a time "in which we breathed . . . // And of each other thought . . . / We thought alike / And that made brothers of us in a home / In which we fed on being brothers . . . ." In the Dutch Church in Kingston, Stevens was impressed by the vision of assembled congregation: "The janitor told me that at one time there were nine judges in the congregation and that often the whole nine of them were there together at a service, sitting in their separate pews," Judge Hasbrouck among them, who left a pamphlet on Spinoza's search for God and the finding of Him "in a predicate of substance." Stevens was impressed. "The material thing," he wrote, "the predicate of substance in this case, was this church: the very building."

I am not about to mount an argument that Stevens in his final years found the answer to philosophic doubt in a return to organized religion. Far from it. But among the inherited figures of imagination, those of Reformed Christianity in Dutch and German Pennsylvania had left a profound and permanent stamp upon his powers of thought and feeling. And in a Dutch Church in Kingston, New York, in the midst of a second world war, Stevens contemplated the power of assembled, rather than solitary, imagination. "Judge Hasbrouck was as well known in Kingston as Martin Luther was in Wittenberg," he writes. And: "He was only one of nine of them, so that, instead of nine judges in the congregation, there were nine poets in the congregation, all of them struggling to get at the predicate of substance. . . ." The struggle is key: this is not a complacent vision. "Turn back to where we were when we began," he writes in the

"Auroras of Autumn," "An unhappy people in a happy world." This has been the great incitement to religious imagination throughout the ages: how to make sense of the gap? Unhappiness in what might as easily have been, might even be except for us, a happy world? "Now, solemnize the secretive syllables," writes the poet, "Read to the congregation." I am alert to the layered ironies. But I am still as stunned by the invoked collective—the congregation—as I am by "innocence." And it has made me realize I need to return with real attention to the late works of Wallace Stevens.

Thinking Versus Imagination

Carl Phillips

"Thought is false happiness," goes the opening of Wallace Stevens's "Crude Foyer":

> Thought is false happiness: the idea
> That merely by thinking one can,
> Or may, penetrate, not may,
> But can, that one is sure to be able—
>
> That there lies at the end of thought
> A foyer of the spirit in a landscape
> Of the mind . . .

Then he proceeds to elaborate on why thought is "false happiness," namely because

> . . . we know that we use
> Only the eye as faculty, that the mind
> Is the eye, and that this landscape of the mind
>
> Is a landscape only of the eye; and that
> We are ignorant men incapable
> Of the least, minor, vital metaphor, content,
> At last, there, when it turns out to be here.

Thinking is apparently—inevitably—false because it is grounded in the literal, as opposed to, presumably, the truer happiness of the figurative, country whose weather is that of "vital metaphor." Thinking versus imagination. Imagination as thinking when the latter refuses groundedness, that is, when it resists the limits of the empirical world, and allows for a world in which "mere" belief is enough to affirm a thing as actual—more specifically, to affirm the metaphorical as actual. And yet, despite the bleak assertions of "Crude Foyer," and in contradiction to that poem's equation of eye and mind, Stevens elsewhere seems to believe that the mind is not only capable of moving beyond the visual, but that the mind is always astir, restless, driven by its impatience with the literal to the truer realm of imagination. As it turns out, "It can never be satisfied, the mind, never," as Stevens says in "The Well Dressed Man with a Beard":

> After the final no there comes a yes
> And on that yes the future world depends.
> No was the night. Yes is this present sun.
> If the rejected things, the things denied,
> Slid over the western cataract, yet one,
> One only, one thing that was firm, even
> No greater than a cricket's horn, no more
> Than a thought to be rehearsed all day, a speech
> Of the self that must sustain itself on speech,
> One thing remaining, infallible, would be
> Enough. Ah! douce campagna of that thing!
> Ah! douce campagna, honey in the heart,
> Green in the body, out of a petty phrase,
> Out of a thing believed, a thing affirmed:
> The form on the pillow humming while one sleeps,
> The aureole above the humming house . . .
>
> It can never be satisfied, the mind, never.

As I understand it, it's not just that the mind can never be satisfied, but that the future *depends* on this lack of satisfaction, satisfaction here being an acceptance of closure, in the form of "no" as rejection, denial. It's the existence of the single thing that *survives* closure that makes all the difference. And notice what happens to this thing: it has only to survive, and it becomes the catalyst for metaphor—first becoming itself a metaphor ("douce campagna of that thing," "honey in the heart"), and then transforming the metaphorical into actuality, merely by being believed in—these at least seem, to me, to be metaphors, conjured out of nowhere, the form on the pillow, the aureole, the humming house, a list that has no end, the ellipsis suggests…

I don't have any firm theories about Stevens's poems, but I have noticed often enough how the expansion of sentence length (along with, frequently, an accompanying increase in syntactic complexity and an intensification of repetition) seems to enact the resistance I'm speaking of, even as it enacts imagination as its own particular *form* of resistance within the presence of possible closure. "The Well Dressed Man with a Beard" begins, for example, with a two-line sentence. Two half-line sentences follow. The next sentence, though, takes up seven lines, and is a sentence marked by heavy repetition: thing/things appears four times, as does the word "one"; "no" appears twice, "speech" does, as well—and in exactly the same line position—"self" is echoed in "itself." Unlike the poem's first three lines, which had a definitive clarity to them—a satisfaction, we might say, with their own thinking–this longer sentence pushes at itself, revises, clarifies, reconsiders, before reaching its end. This is what I mean by restlessness, a restlessness of mind that the sentence itself enacts. After which, the poem tips into the figurative realm, first a one-line fragment ("Ah! douce campagna of that thing!"), then the fragment that follows, of five lines, but also unending–again, the ellipsis, leaving us to drift further into the figurative world, as if forever, except—. Except that there's the final line, one that in tone and in its absoluteness, its closedness to argument, returns us to the colder, more analytic and less expansive realm with which the poem opened. Why?

The ellipsis, the white space and how it leaves that final sentence to exist as its own stanza, in the shadow of the preceding stanza of sixteen lines—Stevens seems to want to emphasize the break, the breach, I'd say, between the figurative world we've just left and the literal one we've been abandoned to, or perhaps to which, from time to time, we are prone to resign ourselves when stripped of imagination. If what I've said about dissatisfaction and how it can lead to imagination is credible, then this final sentence is hopeful in terms of *what* it says. But in terms of *how* it says it, it seems cold, fixed, isolated—and diminished, somehow. "What to make of a diminished thing"—as Frost once wondered, in "The Ovenbird." What, indeed?

If restlessness equals imagination, is stillness a form of thinking, the kind of thinking that, in its being stuck in the literal, translates as false happiness? And yet, how to know either one without the other? Here is "Autumn Refrain":

> The skreak and skritter of evening gone
> And grackles gone and sorrows of the sun,
> The sorrows of sun, too, gone . . . the moon and moon,
> The yellow moon of words about the nightingale
> In measureless measures, not a bird for me
> But the name of a bird and the name of a nameless air
> I have never—shall never hear. And yet beneath
> The stillness of everything gone, and being still,
> Being and sitting still, something resides,
> Some skreaking and skrittering residuum,
> And grates these evasions of the nightingale
> Though I have never—shall never hear that bird.
> And the stillness is in the key, all of it is,
> The stillness is all in the key of that desolate sound.

"Autumn Refrain" opens with a seven-line fragment that uses repetition—of words and of sounds (i.e., assonance and alliteration)—to make associations, a density of repetition that suggests a ruminative mode. The mode of thinking—false happiness. And indeed, the fragment's subject seems grounded in the empirical: the nightingale can't be heard (or seen, presumably), so it can't exist except as word—"not a bird for me / But the name of a bird." But this opening fragment, while addressing the literal, from the start employs the figurative: "skreak and skritter of evening," "sorrows of the sun," "yellow moon of words." Beneath what Stevens will refer to as the "stillness of everything gone," we see as well restlessness of imagination, its impatience with the literal's limitations. And with the Shakespearean turn of "And yet" at line seven (for this seems in its logic very much a Shakespearean sonnet), the repetition that signaled rumination shifts to the repetition of revision—to my mind, a higher register of restlessness than rumination (since, instead of meandering around a thing, there's an effort to push past it): "being still, / Being and sitting still," "something resides, / Some streaking . . . . " Also, at the poem's midpoint, we shift from the relative stasis of fragment to an extended, complex sentence, what we've seen as a form of resistance to stasis—which is to say, we might expect a shift here from thinking to imagination. And this is precisely what happens, slyly, in the poem's closing couplet. The couplet suggests the closure or finality of false happiness—that is, of thinking—both by having both lines anchored in anaphora ("stillness") and also via chiasmus ("key," "all," "all," "key"), that device which tends to suggest a frame, containment, a cage. But the poem ends with the phrase "that desolate sound." The speaker who has "never—shall never hear that bird" manages nevertheless to *imagine* what that bird would sound like, and meanwhile gives a name to the earlier-mentioned "nameless air." And not only does this moment of imagination seem to have emerged as "residuum" from stillness (like the one surviving thing in "The Well Dressed Man with a Beard"), but the imagined is the key that defines the stillness. Otherwise, it's stillness without a backdrop against which to be *understood* as stillness.

Thinking, then, yields imagination? Imagination gives context to thought? Or is it that imagination is the false thing, or maybe more accurately a *falsifying* thing, insofar as it makes of thinking—reality—more than what in fact it is?

In his essay "The Noble Rider and the Sound of Words," Stevens defines the nature of poetry as "an interdependence of the imagination and reality as equals." Reality—thinking—being synonymous with the plain sense of things, from what I can tell from his poem "The Plain Sense of Things":

> After the leaves have fallen, we return
> To a plain sense of things. It is as if
> We had come to an end of the imagination,
> Inanimate in an inert savoir.

It is difficult even to choose the adjective
For this blank cold, this sadness without cause.
The great structure has become a minor house.
No turban walks across the lessened floors.

The greenhouse never so badly needed paint.
The chimney is fifty years old and slants to one side.
A fantastic effort has failed, a repetition
In a repetitiousness of men and flies.

Yet the absence of the imagination had
Itself to be imagined. The great pond,
The plain sense of it, without reflections, leaves,
Mud, water like dirty glass, expressing silence

Of a sort, silence of a rat come out to see,
The great pond and its waste of the lilies, all this
Had to be imagined as an inevitable knowledge,
Required, as a necessity requires.

The interdependence that Stevens speaks about appears early here, in the first stanza. Even as we are told of having returned to the plain sense of things, that state is described first by analogy—"it is as if / We had come to an end of the imagination"—and then imagination is itself described not so plainly, as "Inanimate in an inert savoir," or state of knowing—the less-than-plain phrasing accompanied by a not-so-plain music, given the assonance of all those short i's, the alliteration of "in-". But what is plain enough is the sentence length, for the poem's first three stanzas—all of the sentences staying within two to three lines for the first stanza and a half, and then each sentence being exactly a line long for four consecutive lines, none of which contains any marked caesura. So, do the leaves that, in their falling, reveal the plain sense of things, amount to the foliage of complex syntax, open stanzas, heightened enjambment, and expanded sentence length? We've seen as much in earlier poems, and here, too, it seems to be the case. With the return to the subject of imagination (its absence, anyway) in stanza four, and with the arrival of the "great pond" that seems to get imagined even as Stevens speaks of it (by which I mean how he keeps adding details, and then details to the details), the stanza opens, we have our longest sentence—at seven lines—heavy enjambment, a preponderance of caesuras (i.e., repetition at the level of timing, we might say, and at the level of silence).

"Yet the absence of imagination had / Itself to be imagined." And it would seem that this absence is the pond itself—which is to say, the plain sense of things is made figurative, as if it could only be seen in terms of—in the context of—what it isn't. The necessity that requires, at poem's end, seems to be both things—the necessity of imagination, but also the necessity of the plain sense of things, the false happiness of thought, without which there'd be no need for imagination, if the latter's purpose is to transcend what's plain. Going further, we might say that imagination would not exist without what's plain. Reality becomes catalyst for the restlessness with reality, and this restlessness is imagination in the making—the idea of there being something beyond what's given. In this sense, reality is not just an activity of the most august imagination—as the title of one of Stevens's late poems asserts—but reality is an activator of imagination, which in turn acts upon reality/plainness as a means of making it more than it is—or at least making it briefly, rescuingly, *seem* to be more than it is. Here are some lines from Stevens's "A Clear Day and No Memories":

> Today the air is clear of everything.
> It has no knowledge except of nothingness
> And it flows over us without meanings . . . .

That's what Stevens says. But that's impossible. "Impossible," imagination says.

Does Ripe Fruit Never Fall?

Stanley Plumly

There's that opening moment in the Stevens segment of the old *Voices & Visions* PBS series when one of Stevens's former co-workers at the Hartford Accident and Indemnity Company is asked his impression of his colleague Wallace Stevens. The anonymous questioner is off camera, so that the question appears to be coming from the air. You have to imagine the simplicity of the scene. This co-worker is a genuine Connecticut Yankee—craggy, weather-worn, retired. He's wearing a ball-cap, as I recall, and is sitting in front of a sort of white chipped-paint work shed in what appears to be his backyard. There's a thoughtful pause before the interviewer rephrases his question. Then, after further thought, the old man says, "Waalll," in his sharp Connecticut Yankee kind of drawl, now trying to bring back his memory of Stevens: "Waalll, if you don't count his personal life, I guess you could say he was a happy man."

You have to also remember Stevens's long winter train rides south, far away from hearth and home—his only happy travel in a holiday world—all the way to Key West, where on one notable emotional and likely inebriated February 1936 evening he gets into a fistfight with Ernest Hemingway. Stevens, in fact, breaks his hand on Hemingway's jaw. Stevens is a fair-sized man, but an insurance executive. Hemingway, fair-sized himself, still fancies himself a boxer.

And I'm thinking, too, of Stevens's wife, Elsie, a truly beautiful woman whose sculpted head (by Adolph A. Weinman) became the profile for the Mercury Head dime and the Liberty Standing half-dollar, issued in 1916, 1945, and 1947 respectively. In other words, the intimate, familiar face of one's wife is turned from art into a work of public and commercial artifice, a kind of a cold pastoral indeed, rendered into the terms of Caesar. Somehow, to me, this artifact as fact suggests the evolving possibility of an unhappy, cold marriage, which, by all accounts, was indeed the case. It also suggests the cold coin of intellection, abstraction, and isolation that is too often mistakenly associated with the tone and texture of Stevens's poems.

But in spite of these aesthetic assumptions about Stevens's life and art, he is, I believe, a deeply emotional poet. He probably best fits that category of poet T. S. Eliot is thinking of when he asserts that poetry is an escape from emotion and personality, not their pursuit; but, of course, Eliot adds that one must possess—or repress—emotion and personality in the first place in order to try to escape it. Stevens thrives in that tension.

Two years ago, in a Sunday *New York Times* piece on Stevens at home in Hartford, Jeff Gordimer makes the point of how moved he, Gordimer, is by doing no more than retracing Stevens's famous walk from his grand house on Westerly Terrace to his insurance office downtown, a walk of some modest distance, yet still a distance, and a walk Stevens took every workday. Like Wordsworth—but covering far less territory—Stevens apparently composed in his head while walking, perhaps at a pentameter clip. What, specifically, moves Gordimer is that the walk is now partly paved with slabs of granite—the stone of graves—each of which is engraved with a numbered section of "Thirteen Ways of Looking at a Blackbird."

Is it the gravestone-like engravings themselves that so moves Gordimer, one through thirteen; or is it the poem itself so palpably available, almost step by step, literally underfoot? Gordimer doesn't say. But I would submit that what is moving to Gordimer, and to any sensitive reader of this modern classic, is the way the poem engages the imagination; the way it works the dynamic relationship between the reader and the blackbird itself, both singular and plural; and the way each way of looking at the blackbird resonates as an entity, an evocation, and as a thing in and of itself, without the least hint of explication or apology; and the way each moment in the poem is an enactment of an act of mind making an association, a connection, a discovery, in which the object—the blackbird—is transformed by each of the thirteen different contexts. The order of the thirteen parts adds up too: adds up as a total visual associative narrative; an emotional, impressionistic, tonal progression. Change the order of the parts you change the imagination of the story—and not for the better.

Just which is it that do we prefer: the beauty of inflections or the beauty of innuendoes; the blackbird whistling or just after; the evening snowing or the evening about to snow? And among the twenty snowy mountains, how is it that we can actually see that the only moving thing is the eye of the blackbird? But we do see it. For Stevens, the imagination is the reality of the thing itself, and the reality is the idea—that is, if you can image images as ideas with bodies. What the intellect must suffer the imagination must reconcile: this possibility, it seems to me, is Stevens's heartfelt mission, poem after poem—to reconcile an intellect in conflict with held feeling. The river is moving, the blackbird must be flying. These realities, to the Romantic, are piercing.

Stevens, by his own admission, is a Romantic poet with a capital R. Keats is one of his touchstone sources, most especially in the odes and in those moments in "The Fall of Hyperion: A Dream" when the role of the poet and uses of imagination are questioned and perhaps, by implication, answered. Should poetry—really and truly—help people to live their lives? Or is it the function of the poem to heal? In the first instance, helping people live their lives, it is Stevens speaking; in the second, poetry as a healing force, it is Keats speaking. Both of the poets and both of these questions are about reconciliation: the art of the poem, the artist, and the reader all coming to terms with what will suffice, so long as what suffices vexes us into insight and empathy.

The Keats connection is crucial since it involves Stevens at the heart of his concerns. I find in Stevens's best poetry not only the act of the most brilliant of minds, but more to the point, Stevens's best writing represents the complex acting out of feelings that become the soliloquies of his own interior paramour. Stevens's essential emotional posture is his spiritual isolation at the moment of contemplation; hence, his essential emotional connection—even at his most ironic—is with melancholy, with "Beauty that must die; / And Joy whose hand is ever at his lips / Bidding adieu." The world according to Stevens may at times seem to be nothing more or less than a planet on a table, worthy, to a disinterested eye, of meditative scrutiny, but whatever Stevens is looking at or internalizing, it is a living planet, a warm planet, a, most certainly, blue, even colorful planet. Stevens's secret subject—as opposed to his apparent subject—is more often enough ekphrastic, the world as a work of art, not unlike the artwork that became his wife.

This is true throughout his career, from "Harmonium" to "The Rock"; and no less true of "The Snow Man" and "Thirteen Ways" than of "Madam La Fleurie" and "Final Soliloquy of the Interior Paramour"; and certainly no less true of the greater longer pieces, such as "The Man with the Blue Guitar," "Notes Toward a Supreme Fiction," and "The Auroras of Autumn." For Stevens there is no subject except that first there is the object, the body of the world the spirit comes from, and he treats this body—in its particulars and textures—as the manifestation of every richness it contains, including its contradictions, ambiguities, and choices; and especially including its weathers, its fruit and flowers, its eternal sun, its houses filled with moonlight, and its city dump also filled with moonlight.

Stevens once said that life is an affair of people, and lamented that there were no people in his poems. Well, perhaps not exactly; yet people, their allusive and ghostly attendance, haunt his poems, as much by their excused absences as by their implied presences, whether it be Peter Quince at the clavier, an old philosopher in Rome, a Mrs. Alfred Uruguay, or Stevens's own dead mother. There is a kind of social circle, like a ring of Saturn, circulating at the circumference of the best of his poetry. The euphonic names don't really matter, except, perhaps, for Elsie, who is ultimately, and anonymously, judged as a negative muse, an inspiring but polarizing presence. Thus Stevens's planet may be inhabited by all manner of exotic and extraordinary nature and by bric-a-brac and objet d'art, but the human tragedy is what animates the imagination that brings it all into vivid and vital life.

If lyric poetry is, deeply, about loss, it is also, simultaneously, about its counter-feeling, longing. Stevens's allusive human and natural figures are inextricably linked to the symbolic world of art, to the human interiors and natural correlatives art speaks to and from. Stevens's blackbird may be his Keatsian nightingale, but his "Sunday Morning"—as just one salient example—is his Keatsian "Ode on a Grecian Urn," in which representative figures of life as art and art as life are treated to paradise in a vexed secular vision. The funereal urn is circular: you turn it in its full three dimensions in the mind and its frozen "happy" pastoral scenes—painted on or in relief–are revealed to be both beautiful and terrifying, since its trees can never change to autumn "nor ever bid the Spring adieu" and its lovers never can quite kiss, "Though winning near the goal." Heaven, in both Keats and Stevens, becomes a hell of permanence, where ripe fruit never falls. Yet we seem to long for such states of permanent being—or do we? T. S. Eliot says that the tragedy of human life is that we can imagine a fulfillment we can never have. It is the tease of transcendence that is part of the price of imagination. In Stevens, no less than Keats, this condition is the tension in their intensity.

"Is there no change of death in paradise?" The wonderful thing about "Sunday Morning" is how filled it is with life as opposed to an after-life. The after-life in this poem performs as this looming presence defined by its absence, such as "Things to be cherished like the thought of heaven." But it's the earth, the mundane, the diurnal, the sweet dailiness of a Sunday morning that blesses us here: the complacencies of the peignoir, the late coffee and oranges, the green freedom of the cockatoo, the calm that darkens among water-lights: these are the earthly details that inform this reality against the old encroachments of "The holy hush of ancient sacrifice." This wholly aesthetic-minded poem builds from this opening stanza to a perception of "Emotions on wet roads on autumn nights" through to the image of "silken weavings of our afternoons" and finally to the lofty fantasy of pagan gods dancing naked in "Their boisterous devotion to the sun." "Their chant shall be a chant of paradise, / Out of their blood." Stevens makes no buried bones about where his passions lie—right at the level of the dew that greets the mortal morning.

In "Sunday Morning," even Jesus lies in his grave—at least, he did; anyway, "The tomb in Palestine / Is not the porch of spirits lingering": it is a house in ruins, because "We live in an old chaos of the sun / Or old dependency of day and night, / Or island solitude." This last reference, especially, represents the place that Stevens's voice is calling from: his island solitude. I cannot think of a lonelier poet among his great generation than Wallace Stevens. His elaborations and attenuations of beauty and truth in his poetry not only enlarge the dimensions of his greatness, they underwrite, no, underscore the burden of tragedy he brings to his work, though "tragedy" may be a borrowed word here: Stevens, like his Beckett-like man on the dump, is "full of images" in search of correspondences—even, perhaps, a correspondent—in search of a dialectic—perhaps a dialogue—that will create a synthesis, a resolution beyond reconciliation. The condition of needing a resolution beyond reconciliation is the longing in his poems. His imagination is filled with possibilities: "Did the nightingale torture the ear, / Pack the heart and scratch the mind?" Yes, it did. I think for this poet Keats's nightingale also packed the heart, as do all those frozen figures on the urn and all those personal ghosts on the peripheries of his vision. "Where was it," Stevens asks, at last, that "one first heard of the truth?" His mortal answer is in the ellipsis following "The the," the real and very definite article.

Marianne Moore

MARIANNE MOORE ANEW

Moore & Less

Stanley Plumly

Of that great American poetry generation born in the 1880s, a generation that includes William Carlos Williams, Ezra Pound, and T. S. Eliot, Marianne Moore is an anomaly: at eye- and ground-level she is no less an influential practitioner of the art of the modernist poem than any of her male contemporaries. It could be argued, in fact, that as a master of specific metaphor and analogue, as an originator of the use of found and exotic material integral to the texture of a poem, as a player with language for its own sake, and as a metaphysician of what unifies yet puzzles a poem, Moore stands out.

There was a time when Moore's contemporary critics wished to ghettoize her surprising style as too often playful and experimental entertainments, as too often elaborations of data and instruction, as too often poetry structures yoked into arbitrary, self-conscious forms, with a penchant for inventive rhymes in which a "Chameleon" sports with "laid upon," "Nineveh" with "Jonah," and, in "The Fish," the hard, hyphenated "ac" sound at the beginning of "accident" is perfect with "lack." Showy stuff. And then there was the issue of syllabics versus metrics, syllable count versus accents, so much so that Moore's so-called "music" called attention to itself—if not as an aural language then as a written word, suggesting, in Robert Lowell's formulation, that Moore "is an inventor of a new kind of English poem, one that is able to fix the splendor and variety of prose in very compressed spaces." A poetry, in other words, that is really compressed prose, with all the knowledgeable range available to prose. Moore herself had once said that "I realized that the spoken word is different from the one on the page."

Otherwise, Moore, in the old days, was being praised for her colorfulness—that is, for her arresting imagery, her love of *objets d'art*, her habit of bric-a-brac, her odd animals treated as familiars and her familiar animals treated as oddments. And then there are the lists, as if researched from the public library; and then a poem like "The Octopus," sustained for about two hundred lines by speculation and quotation and outré reference. Plus a personal poetry biography that invites the Brooklyn Dodgers, *Life* magazine, the Ford Motor Company into the sacred temple of the arena of the poem; and then the funny hat, the cape, and life at home still with your mother. In sum: Moore is to be characterized as the poet as eccentric yet popular, as different but finally chummy.

Even if all of this, in total, is only half-true—which it is—it is all beside the point of Moore's greatness, her contribution, and her influence, one essential quality of which is her best poetry's paying attention to what I think of as the art of silence, the art of the means to achieve an abiding *ars poetica* of the modest self: Moore's silences being but one vital aspect of her writing that may seem miles away from her apparent and abundant method, interest, and obsession. For instance, big poems such as "The Octopus," "The Pangolin," and "In Distrust of Merits"—all anthology pieces—would seem to argue, demonstratively, against what is implied by silence. These poems are filled with complicating rhetoric and logic, wide-eyed lines and off-balance line-breaks, a massive sense of space occupied, and a "rough music" of insistence underscored by the angularity of syllabics (syllabics being a concept Moore refused, early on, to talk about). Yet even in these samples there are silences, absences, separations that cause or imply connection; and there is the commitment of a mind that believes that what is left out will, by the reader, be filled in.

"The Octopus" is one long seminal progression that seems to want to smother the reader with information, evocation, and as many tentacles as possible, but there is one willy-nilly stanza break, which acts like a breather, near the end of the poem, and several other silent breaks within the developing text. It is a greedy poem, gathering in as much imaginative and associative possibilities as seems possible—very like an octopus. Yet for all its acquisitional and collective power, the poem stops and restarts constantly; it moves here, then there; it quotes as if to interrupt as much as reinforce its speaker. It distracts and deflects its potential straight-line narrative.

All of which is to say: it gives pause as often as it can and turns away from transition. It fills itself, so to speak, with separations and absences.

"In Distrust of Merits," like "The Pangolin," builds itself with evenhanded but consistently enjambing stanzas; rather than a recitation, it is, however, a meditation in a time of war, published first in *The Nation* in 1943. It analogizes both the Old and New Testaments to construct its plea for tolerance and humanity as an antidote opposed to the isolation of self-destruction that war represents, in which the "world's an orphan's home." Ultimately, this poem is a Keatsian assertion of the fact that "Beauty is everlasting / and dust"—and the poet here means for us to rhyme a silent "us" with "dust"—"Beauty is everlasting / and dust is for a time." The poem's stanza-breaks, regardless of its pushy enjambments, are, of course, visual as well as vocal silences, but it is the movement of the "enchanted" mind—in and out, over and across spaces of reference—that creates Moore's necessary and intensifying suspensions and arrivals over the course of eighty lines. And at the close of her poem, it is her moral acceptance of another kind of silence that elevates Moore's argument for art to the terms of beauty—"inwardly," she says, "I . . . did nothing" against the war but write a poem.

When Moore was asked why she reduced one of her most famous poems, "Poetry," to just three lines from its original thirty full lines of five stanzas, her answer was that she felt, on reflection, that after the first two sentences the poem was over—or, more precisely, that the rest was "padding." She might well have said that the rest of the poem—that is, the remaining twenty-seven lines—required silence, since silence is another way to look at what was there and now should not be there. Silence, in this case, being an absent presence. The good thing, in hindsight, is that we have both versions of the poem and can test what Moore thinks silence is: i.e., a subtraction; or an anti-addition. Without the missing or silent lines we lose not only her argument but her discovery and juxtaposition of quotations from a sagacious Yeats and a didactic Tolstoy regarding what Moore pretends poetry is and is not: is it imagination versus business documents; or, is it a combination and inevitable connection of things, apparently disparate things, within a compatible world?—even in terms of different levels of reality, such as imaginary gardens with real toads in them. How compatible should these connections be? How far apart, how "surreal"? Wallace Stevens's complaint against surrealism is that it is too much like clams playing the accordion, yet, when you picture it, as you might in a Moore poem, this undersea image makes a certain visual sense.

But playful is one thing, serious another. Moore's powerful one-page poem "A Grave"—originally titled "A Graveyard"—invites an absence right off the bat. It begins with a de-articled "Man looking into the sea" rather than "a man" or "the man" or "some man." Man alone and at large has the feeling of mankind, yet I think Moore is interested less in a universal than in an archetypal representative whose specific role seems to be that of a great meditative presence so present as to block the view:

> Man looking into the sea,
> taking the view from those who have as much right to see it as
> you have to it yourself,
> it is human nature to stand in the middle of a thing,
> but you cannot stand in the middle of this;
> the sea has nothing to give but a well excavated grave.

The elided leap from the shoreline into the sea itself is itself a silence in that the step from the one to the other is not only subtracted but necessary. The referent for "this" is in both places—the shore and the sea—at once, and serves to rescue the difference between standing by and standing in this most massive of all graves. Man, therefore, is looking into the Grave. The seventeen long lines that follow these first five separate into semicolons, dashes, colons, and periods that may help organize the space of the poem: They also, however, release it, free it, in effect, into a logic of juxtapositions in which Moore can keep us at the edge while exploring the sea-life of death—as if death finally means to go under, down, sunk in a drift "in which all dropped things are bound to sink— / in which if they turn and twist, it is neither with volition nor consciousness."

The ongoing back-and-forth between our position in life on land and death among the fishes, seaweed, "tortoise-shell scourges," and so on, evokes the tension that is what the source of imagination is about. Men may row above, cast their nets into, build their lighthouses near this grave that is the sea, but to no avail. The tension in the silence between—or within—land and sea, surface and the deep is the content here. "Man" is all of us, genderless, fishers of men, fishermen all. And this grave, this all-depth of water, is as beautiful as it is dark:

> The wrinkles progress among themselves in a phalanx—
>   beautiful under networks of foam,
> and fade breathlessly while the sea rustles in and out of the seaweed;
> the birds swim through the air at top speed, emitting cat-calls as
>   heretofore— .

Wonderful that pun on "swim"; remarkable the power in "top speed, emitting cat-calls as heretofore"—no speed, no cat-calls hereafter.

Silence, for Moore, seems to be less about imaginative leaps of faith or the rawness of the raw materials than about not staying beyond your welcome. As such it is a distancing device, promoting what Keats, after Hazlitt, calls disinterestedness, which is yet another way to disappear, with reticence, behind the text. Moore's work, therefore, is as much about definition as it is about delineation, which in itself demands the work of poetic economy. Her understatement is a form of denial in favor of an alternative richness. Her poet's job is to take away expectation, reverse the scale of the expected, let the air out of the large and give a touch of the grand to the small—glaciers become octopi, snakes make modesty a virtue. For example, unlike her contemporary D. H. Lawrence, she does not treat her animal encounters as passional subjects but as inspiring objects to be viewed outside the outlines of elevated narrative and instead inside the circle of a configuration, an approximation, a comparison, as if she were a kind of cubist seeing the animal in the round and thereby transforming it.

When I read a really fine and moving poem by Moore, a poem such as "A Grave" or "In Distrust of Merits," I feel I am in a very intimate, almost private place—a space, if you will, of profound solitude: this, too, is a silence. The paradox is, it seems to me, that such a singular, separate place is not isolating but comforting, connecting, as personal to the reader as it is to the writer—one silence, as Rilke puts it, speaking to another silence. Moore's poem entitled "Silence" sets the case pretty well. It is set itself in an older, conservative, perhaps more silent Cambridge, Massachusetts:

> My father used to say,
> "Superior people never make long visits,
> have to be shown Longfellow's grave
> or the glass flowers at Harvard.
> Self-reliant like the cat—
> that takes its prey to privacy,
> the mouse's limp tail hanging like a shoelace from its mouth—
> they sometimes enjoy solitude,
> and can be robbed of speech
> by speech which has delighted them.
> The deepest feeling always shows itself in silence;
> not in silence, but restraint."
> Nor was he insincere in saying, "Make my house your inn."
> Inns are not residences.

It is generally best when the thing speaks for itself. "Silence" here speaks for itself—or, rather, Moore allows the father figure literally to speak for her about silence, about privacy and solitude and not overstaying your welcome; and especially about how authentic feeling "shows itself" in the tension of holding back, of listening, of creating spaces within the space. Moore's "silence" in the presence of the father puts her in the position of the listener, the learner, and the daughter superior. Her active role is to hear, and—in the words of St. Mark—to understand. Silence builds the structure of the insight, whose artful construction is exactly what the overall forms of Moore's poems are about: constructs of subtraction in tension with assertion. Silences, that is, controlled by the larger silent white space of the page. Silence, in fact, Moore seems to be saying, is about listening to that space, is about letting it speak for itself.

Thinking about Thinking in Marianne Moore

LINDA GREGERSON

In October of 1961, there appeared in the pages of *Harper's Bazaar* a prose "fantasy" by Marianne Moore entitled "My Crow, Pluto" (*Complete Prose,* 556-58). "I had always wanted a crow," she writes, "and received a mechanical one for Christmas. Then Pluto, whose rookery is in Fort Green Park about a block from me, adopted me—a dream come true." Pluto, Moore reports, "was fanatically interested in detail," and appeared to share other predilections with the poet as well, displaying a decided appreciation for honey, watercress, buckwheat cakes and dehydrated alfalfa as well as the resident typewriter and Doctor Zulli's broadcast lectures on "Landmarks in the Evolution of the Novel." "He understood me," writes Moore, "and I him from the first" and supports that assertion with a series of increasingly improbable anecdotes about their domestic communication.

On the facing page of the same issue of *Harper's Bazaar,* Pluto reigns as subject and interlocutor in a poem whose formal proposition is so extreme as to be nearly perverse. Lines of two syllables, stanzas of two lines, rhymed. And O, a monorhyme.

TO VICTOR HUGO OF MY CROW PLUTO

"Even when the bird is walking we know that it has wings."
—Victor Hugo

Of:
my crow
Pluto,

the true
Plato

azzurro-
negro

green-blue
        rainbow —

Victor Hugo,
it is true

we know
that the crow

"has wings," how-
ever pigeon-toe-

inturned on grass. We do.
                    (adagio)

As the mechanical crow in the prose narrative had the power to conjure into being an actual crow from Fort Green Park, so the flagrant mechanics of prosody have the power to conjure into being a field of sympathetic understanding between bird and poet. Victor Hugo appears to have gained entry into this choice company as much for the felicitous syllabics and terminal vowel sound that constitute his name as for the sentiment expressed in the epigraph, which he contributes: "Even when the bird is walking we know that it has wings." Victor Hugo does not stay around for long.

After the *adagio*—(ad - agio means "at ease" or "slowly." And what is it, exactly, that moves at such an easy pace? The bird on the grass? The bird in the air? The mind in pursuit of the bird?)—after the adagio, Victor Hugo is summarily dispensed with and the place of second person awarded to the crow, to whom it rightfully belongs. And though the stock of terminal o-sounds in English quickly runs low, by a happy coincidence bird and poet find they share a language quite like the Italian, rich in terminal o's. (And for those of us who are slow to acquire new languages, the author kindly supplies a glossary in crow-esperanto at the bottom of her poem—see below).

Vivo-
rosso

"corvo,"
although

con dizio-
nario

io parlo
Italiano–

this pseudo
Esperanto

which, savio
ucello

you speak too –
my vow and motto

(botto e tottot)
io giuro

è questo
credo:

lucro
è peso morto.

"Lucro è peso morto": profit is a dead weight, a phrase the poet found in her Italian dictionary, as she confesses in another prose-piece written for profit. This one appeared in March of 1963 in the pages of *Seventeen* magazine. Its stance is explicitly moralizing: "greed seems to me," writes Moore, "the vice of our century" (*Complete Prose*, 568). A sentiment I keep hoping will help me understand the pivot point of the poem she published two years earlier. "And so," as though what follows will be the necessary correlate of an axiomatic truth.

> And so
> dear crow—
>
> gioièllo
> mio—
>
> I have to
> let you go;
>
> a bel bosco
> generoso,
>
> tuttuto
> vagabondo,
>
> serafino
> uvaceo
>
> Sunto,
> oltremarino
>
> verecondo
> Plato, adio.

In addition to poem and prose narrative, the author compiled what she called "impromptu equivalents for *esperanto madinusa* (made in U.S.A) for those who might not resent them":

azzuro-negro: blue-black	gioièllo mio: my jewel
vivorosso: lively	a bel bosco: to lovely woods
con dizionario: with dictionary	tuttuto vagabondo: complete gypsy
savio ucello: knowing bird	serafino uvaceo: grape-black seraph
io giuro: I swear	sunto: in short
è questo credo: is this credo	verecondo: modest

lucro è peso morto: profit is a dead weight

And so, writes the poet, I let you go. From what logical maneuver exactly does this resolution proceed? One might imagine that a thinking person would need no more than Victor Hugo to show her where to go: "Even when the bird is walking we know that it has wings." Those wings alone, their aptitude for flight, their sheer stored potential and our knowing it, ought to provide the adequate principle: don't trap a winged thing on the ground. But that would not require a poem. Moore was meticulous in her insistence that a poem must earn its way, that it constitute "invention" in the rigorous, double, Renaissance sense of the word: invention as making or devising, as in the modern sense, and also invention as a seeking out of that which preexists or exceeds the power of will. The poem must be a marriage of contrivance and surrender.

What is it that "To Victor Hugo of My Crow Pluto" contrives, and comes upon, that its epigraph alone does not provide? *Lucro è peso morto*. Profit and its corollary, greed. The profit is that heady flight of virtuosity in which Pluto, the blue-black powers of darkness, and Plato, philosopher of forms, are conscripted for service to the poet's fantasy of unimpeded apprehension. "He understood me, and I him from the first." Which is to say, he was "my" crow: apprehension of this masterful sort is proprietary and thus a form of greed. The human envies the bird his wings. But "we should exemplify what we require of others," writes Moore in the prose-piece "Pluto," "and, having badgered a neighbor into returning a racoon to the woods where he got it, I asked one day, 'Pluto, where were you born?' He said what sounded like 'Correct account.'" Connecticut? The poet ventures and, receiving what she takes to be an affirmative reply, releases her crow in the Connecticut woods. The letting go cannot happen preemptively. Victor Hugo supplies the principle but not the passage through, the lively—*vivorosso*—graspingness. To be sure, the wild display of pseudo Esperanto put through its paces on the highwire of dimeter couplets innoculates the poem quite well against mere earnestness. But play can be greedy too. The poem becomes an exquisite device for having-it and giving-it-up-for-profit too, which is to say, for the mantle of virtue.

The poem tells us too, I would argue, something about what thinking is meant to feel like in a poem by Marianne Moore. Moore once said of Wallace Stevens that "his repercussive harmonics . . . 'prove' mathematically" (*Complete Prose*, 347). "Correct account," says Pluto, the crow, and the working out of prosodic proposition, however preposterous, like the working out of an ethical problem, has for Moore the step-by-step pragmatism, and the stunning imaginative leaps, of math. "And what are worthy ends?" she asks in 1963, in the magazine essay for teenage girls. Two things, the poet answers: "Knowledge made possible by an overpowering desire to possess it," which is to say, greed of the allowable sort. And "usefulness," like "the ether mask," whose inventor, foregoing profit, refused to patent the device so that it might be available to all who needed it. "One would like," writes Moore, "to have invented the zipper fastener, epoxy glue, the collapsible dustpan, figure-eight stitch closure of the hide cover of the baseball." Which practical things sound very like the poetry of T. S. Eliot as described by Marianne Moore, a poetry in which "concepts and images are toothed together."

In an effort to escape the inadequacies of "brain-bound thinking," cognitive psychologists have posited a phenomenon called "distributed cognition" and the related phenomenon of "extended mind," which "depends . . . on" and incorporates "the ongoing work of the body and /or extra-organismic environment." Andy Clark, one of the leading theorists in this realm, has referred in *Supersizing the Mind* to the extended mind as a "natural-born cyborg": "it is our basic human nature," he writes, "to annex, exploit and incorporate nonbiological stuff deep into our mental profiles." (Clark, *Natural-Born Cyborgs*). Essential to this theory, in other words, is its universality: we all possess or participate in extended mind. The classic example of distributed cognition is Edwin Hutchins's account, in *Cognition in the Wild*, of eighteenth century warship navigation, maneuvers far too intricate and emergent to be accomplished by a single brain-bound organism. In another realm, in "Distributing Cognition in the Globe," Elizabeth Tribble has proposed distributed cognition as a key to Elizabeth stage practice, where actors were required to keep "a staggering number of plays" in repertory with only cue-scripts and schematic plots to guide them. John Sutton, the clinical psychologist, has assembled in "Distributed Cognition: Domains and Dimensions" a wonderfully cogent taxonomy of the social, technological, symbolic, and biological resources that supplement the human brain to constitute extended mind. These concepts and all that they suggest for an expanded view of memory, pattern, and problem solving seem to me to capture something fundamental to Moore's philosophy-in-action, which is to say, her poems. In earlier eras, one might have called this thinking-that's-larger-than-we-are God or, under a different regime, the Muse. Others have called it Nature. Despite her inexhaustible enchantment with nature, however, that old-fashioned name for sovereign principle doesn't quite capture Moore's invocations of system, which include what we call nature but also the realms of human and technological ingenuity. She does not disdain the zipper. Nor geometry.

An icosahedron is a geometric figure with twenty faces, each of them an equilateral triangle, each triangle congruent with three others, five triangles meeting at each vertex of the polyhedron. These regularities and congruencies make it, in Euclidean geometry, one of the five Platonic solids.

THE ICOSASPHERE

"In Buckinghamshire hedgerows
the birds nesting in the merged green density
weave little bits of string and moths and feathers and thistledown,
in parabolic concentric curves" and,
working for concavity, leave spherical feats of rare efficiency;
whereas through lack of integration,

avid for someone's fortune,
three were slain and ten committed perjury,
six died, two killed themselves, and two paid fines for risks they'd
run.
But then there is the icosasphere
in which at last we have steel-cutting at its summit of economy,
since twenty triangles conjoined can wrap one

ball or double-rounded shell
with almost no waste, so geometrically
neat, it's an icosahedron. Would the engineers making one,
or Mr. J. O. Jackson, tell us
how the Egyptians could have set up seventy-eight-foot solid
granite vertically?
We should like to know how that was done.

When she published this poem in book form, the author kindly supplied three notes. In one she attributes the quotation about Buckinghamshire hedgerows to E. McKnight Kauffer, whom I discover to have been an expatriate American graphic designer of eclectic idiom, incorporating cubist, vorticist, futurist, and, presumably, hedgerow influences, and most famous for a series of 140 posters he produced for the London Underground. In the second note, Moore explains those dreadful casualties in stanza two as fallout from a Dickensian dispute among claimants for the $30,000,000 snuff fortune of Mrs. Henrietta Edwardina Schaefer Garrett, who died intestate, as reported in *The New York Times*. In the third note, Moore identifies J. O. Jackson as the inventor of a brilliant new design for the assembly of steel globes "with negligible scrap loss." Three notes, three instances, linked by likeness and inversion. Whereas. But then.

Without the aid of calculus, and with methods very like the poet's—incorporating bits of string and moths and thistledown and excerpts from *The New York Times*—the bird in the hedgerow produces a spherical nest of dazzling mathematical precision. Whereas, through greed and lack of integration, aspirant heirs to a snuff fortune drop like flies. Integration is a mathematical term; indeed, it is one of the fundamental concepts of calculus and has many practical applications, such as determining the volume of a solid or the area beneath a curve. In 1949, *The New York Times* reported some 25,990 claimants to Mrs. Garrett's fortune. What's 30,000,000 divided by 25,990 times x (surely there were lawyers) minus three minus ten minus six minus two times two? Considerable waste. But then: the ingenious solution to a vexing engineering problem: a method for assembling spheres from flat-cut polyhedrons. Why twenty-sided? Wouldn't a hundred and twenty be yet more precise? Because twenty equilateral triangles represents "the greatest number of regular sides geometrically possible"—the icosahedron represents the outer limit of Platonic forms.

I do not think Moore means any disrespect to Mr. J. O. Jackson when she poses her question about the Egyptians. Moore values designers and engineers. Nor is she a skeptic about progress: she celebrates the zipper and the ether mask. Her faith in the worthy products of modern brain-bound ingenuity is only exceeded by her faith—her rapturous faith—in the workings of extended mind. The icosasphere is wonderful precisely because it is of a piece with the bird's nest and the lost contrivances of ancient Egyptian engineers. The bird is knowing—*savio*—too. And gene by gene, generation by generation, enacts a knowing that is larger than itself.

We may have said too often and too lightly that poems can "think." But we've all had the experience of fretting over syntax or syllable count or echoing vowel sounds while something more ineffable—some working-out of affect or ethics or analogy—appears to proceed on its own. The Renaissance had it right about invention: the trail-blazer is always a follower too. When mathematicians "discover" the solution to a complex problem, they understand their work not as adding something new to the fabric of the universe but rather as revealing something that has a priori status. The materiality of language incites the poet to discovery because it also holds her to account, and this despite the fact, or in addition to the fact, that language is itself a perpetually evolving form of scaffolding. Form is the poet's prosthetic thinking-machine, "a puzzle," as Moore once wrote about the music of Stravinsky, "in the perfection of hoarded intentionalness" (*Complete Prose,* 543). The boundaries between self and world are vanishingly thin. And poems can be smarter than we are.

Almost Utmost: Marianne Moore

David Baker

Who is stranger than Marianne Moore? Whose poems are more packed with eccentricity and oddity and ubiquitous impunity? She'd love those words. The strange is her familiar, as the just-discovered is her comfort, and the said-only-once-and-only-this-way is her residential idiom. She measured with her mind's eye and made the utmost rapturous music. She tried to name a car and nominated a whole new species of weirdness instead—and kept the money. She wore white gloves and tricorn hats and wrote the liner notes for *I Am the Greatest!*, Mohammad Ali's spoken-word record. Did you know Marianne Moore threw out the first ball on opening day, Yankee Stadium, in 1968?

Exactly two hundred years earlier, in 1668, a young Puritan teacher, on a sea voyage from England to find a home in the new world, leaned over the ship rail to observe how "a pair of sunfish lie flapping on the water." In a characteristic combination of scientific curiosity and religious over-determination, he adds that "they say this kind of fish is thus that it cannot sink while the sun shines." Two hundred and sixty-nine years later, in 1937, while working at the Yale library, Thomas Johnson (whom we know as the editor of Emily Dickinson's poetry, the heroic one who restored her work to its first idiosyncratic formats) discovered more than 7,000 pages of poetry by this forgotten man and gave back to the world the poems of Edward Taylor, still in his handmade leather binders. For nearly sixty years Taylor had lived in the wild-west frontier of Westfield, Massachusetts, its minister, its village doctor, likely a farmer, and wrote poems all along. Also in 1937, writing to a "Mr. Stevens" to praise his *Man with the Blue Guitar*, Marianne Moore asserts that "as music is best described by performing it, poetry is best defined by writing it." I am certain that Moore's famous fish, who "wade through black jade," are of the same species as Taylor's magic fish who lie flapping on top of the sea.

There's a brand of American poet, American Adventurer, for whom the frontier is as interior as it is outer: both literal and littoral, strange, roiling, populated with demons and tricksters and angels and all manner of new critters. For whom the only acceptable language must be just as tweaked, as peaked or flushed with wildness as the subject may require. For whom measurement is part of the mapping, naming is part of the blessing, and blessing—in the form of the ode or the curse or the prayer or the metaphysical gallop—is the name of the art. Edward Taylor. Emily Dickinson. Or from her time, Wallace Stevens and E. E. Cummings (whom Moore calls in a letter to *him,* "blasphemous, inexorable, disrespectful, sinful author"). Marianne Moore counts in the company of the rarest birds of American poetic imagination and invention.

An explorer's first task—after survival—is to map, to record. My father was a land surveyor. When I turned fourteen, he taught me how to hold and wave the tall rod, how to sight hash-marks through the geodolite, how to record the contours, step by step, of the land, and how to convert those figures into the artful geometry of a topographic map. Chaos, the wild, turns into terrain. Moore is a mapper of the strange.

I want to look at two poems of Moore's to show her method of mapping and its achievements and to examine her naturalist's sense of discovery and nomination. As Grace Schulman asserts, "to read a poem by Marianne Moore is to be aware of exactitude. It is to know that the writer has looked at a subject—a cliff, a sea animal, an ostrich—from all sides, and has examined the person looking at it as well."

"Melchior Vulpius" shows Moore looking (and listening) closely indeed and responding with great admiration as both mapper and namer to her subject at hand. She notes his dates as 1560-1615, and commences her poem by identifying him as a "contrapuntalist" and composer of hymns and anthems:

We have to trust this art—
                                        this mastery which none

can understand. Yet someone has
acquired it and is able to
  direct it. Mouse-skin-bellows'-breath
  expanding into rapture saith

"Hallelujah." Almost
                    utmost absolutist
and fugue-ist, Amen; slowly building
from miniature thunder,
  crescendos antidoting death—
  love's signature cementing faith.

The hortatory, the odic, must be counted as one of Moore's pressing rhetorical impulses. This is a poet of celebratory invention. When a poet writes an ode, a poem heightened by praise, it's worth noting not only those traits the poet sets out to praise but the subject itself. The *choice* of subject tells us about the artist; she shows us important contours in the terrain of her own values. Just look at portraits of Moore's modernist peers: the fantastically named fictives of Stevens (as in the racist exotica of Chieftain Iffucan or "pale Ramon," or the shrugged-off "so-and-so" Mrs. Pappadopoulos); on the other hand, the unnamed or dis-identifying "une femme" of Pound and the mere "lady" of Eliot. Moore loves the names, the ascertaining features, of the actual and present, "the thing itself," as Maureen McLane says about her, "and the idea about the thing."

So why Melchior Vulpius? He was a German composer, a singer of hymns, cantor of church music, who wrote hundreds of songs and published two books of Latin *Cantiones sacrae* as well as *Lateinische Hochzeitstücke*. Moore gets his birth year wrong—1670, not 1660—but is exacting in her survey of his music, those "wedding-hymns to Latin words." Praise is nothing if not a most devout species of attention. Look at the way her poem lays out on the page, typical of the intricate design of her poems, the "scaled specificity," in McLane's good phrase. It looks like a little map; a blueprint; a score. It looks a little messy at first, inkblot, until we begin to discern the design. As a sidenote, I'll add that the poem with its sort-of six-line stanzas and its couplet rhyme at the end of each also replicates the form of nearly all of Edward Taylor's own metaphysical devotional poems.

As in so many of her rich poems, Moore makes a shape out of the chaotic. The broken, indented, uneven first stanza finds the contours of its form on repetition. Moore makes snowflakes, fractals—uneven shapes that become formal designs upon redundancy. Accident (that important word in "The Fish") becomes shapeliness; an architecture emerges from an evolving form. For Moore the broken becomes baroque.

Here is Vulpius's hymn:

> Now God be praised in heaven above,
> Praised be He for His great love,
> Wherein all creatures live and move,
> Hallelujah! (Hallelujah!)
>
> Now God be praised for conquering faith,
> Which feareth neither pain nor death,
> But trusting God, rejoicing saith,
> Hallelujah! (Hallelujah!)
>
> His grace defends us from all ill;
> His Christ shall be our leader still
> Till heaven and earth shall do His will,
> Hallelujah! (Hallelujah!)

Vulpius was a Lutheran, and Moore a good Presbyterian who could be found most Sundays at the Lafayette Avenue Presbyterian Church of Brooklyn. That's where she heard this song and copied it out by hand onto her church bulletin, dated June 3, 1957. (She switched the order of Vulpius's first two stanzas, by the way.)

Look what else she carries over from his hymn to hers. His rhyming, in triplets, recurs in her terminal couplets, as well as in the abounding internal rhymes she so much delights in: "hymns" and "anthem"; "Mouse-skin," "Amen"; "absolutist and fugue-ist," with its further pun as both a personification and a superlative. But more about that rhyme, the logic of that rhyme: as George Steiner says of Paul Valery, "reason bids the poet prefer rhyme to reason." Here the *rhyme* of "saith" also leads us pointedly to its second sonic characteristic, its *metrical* feature. I would say "saith" in two syllables (SAY-eth), a trochee. But in context of this rhyme, and as Vulpius does, the dominating "faith" mandates only a single pulse for "saith," to get the rhyme right. That is, the pronunciation of "saith" in one *syllable* also nudges it closer to an exact *rhyme* with "faith." And look at Vulpius's text again, at the second stanza (which she transposed as first) where those three rhymes reside, the exact words that Moore picks up and repositions in her three terminal couplets.

Consider Moore's further thinking-this-through. Her first stanza's couplet both names and demonstrates the narrative crisis of the poem: The threat to faith, the thing that might "conquer" faith, is "death," which comes last. But faith can be—to a true believer, and through the mastery of artful, rapturous song—ultimately itself the "conquering" thing. To show this, she flips their positions in the third stanza. Thus, in a reversal, a kind of cognitive irony, she demonstrates that faith wins; it cements its immortality through love, signing it, getting, as it were, the last word in.

I think of that flip, that ironic reversal, as a kind of formal counterpoint. Isn't her subject itself, Melchior Vulpius, first identified as a "contrapuntalist"? Isn't his musical mastery precisely the thing Moore admires in his work? We know that counterpoint is one of the dominant features of the baroque fugue. A song made of changing or different keys, or rhythms, or phrasal movements: irony, in Harold Bloom's definition, is the clash of incommensurate forces. *This* movement is intersected by *that* movement; a crossing-over or -under of entities; at the crux, thus, a crisis. Here counterpoint literally enacts a crisis of faith and finds its resolution in faith's conquering power.

But I want to look at Moore's further contrapuntal aesthetic. This is my primary point about her style in poem after poem. We identify Marianne Moore as one of the great exemplars of syllabic poetry. She counts her single syllables obsessively—though in conversation with Grace Schulman she disavowed that stance with a stern "Syllabics? Oh, I repudiate that." The history of our art in English tends to evolve, though, *not* out of syllabics, but out of accentuals, a counting of heavy pulses. Poetry tends to evolve out of sonic or musical features. I have never heard a single poet—except for Richard Wilbur, whom I believe—claim to be able actually to hear syllabics as a metric. We hear downbeats. We HEAR DOWN-beats, and we measure the length of lines by the number and relative position of those heavy beats and light beats. Perhaps such an audible rhythm facilitates not just our delight but our memory. Rhyme, too, is a feature of the mnemonic. Even our first poem shows the point I'm making. The youngster sings "A-b C-d E-f GEEE / H-i J-k Lmno PEEE." The syllable count in those two rhythmic units differs notably, but the four downbeats are unmistakable—and dominate. Thus the two phrasal units sound, they *feel*, equivalent.

I have this notion that syllabics evolves more substantially in poetry as poetry becomes less an oral art and more a written or textualized art. Singing leads to accentuals. Reading leads to syllabics. That is, syllabics is a written evolution of an oral art, where the metrics of rhythm is converted, by the alchemy of printing, into the meter of mere numbers, numbers seen rather than numbers heard. But with Moore, mere numbers are their own elegance; they can enact, as Steiner puts it, "the music to mathematics."

"Melchior Vulpius" is an example of Marianne Moore's expression of formal counterpoint. One line of expression comes through the quantitative syllabic duration of the poem: 6 6 8 7 8 8, to look at the first stanza. The other line of expression is the distinctly varying accentual contour of the lines of the poem. Syllabics plays counterpoint to the accentual meter, rather than, as in our normative accentual-syllabic meter, syllables and accents working in regular concert. Look at the three first lines here, their meter: "a CONtraPUNtalIST," with three iambs. "We HAVE to TRUST this ART," also iambic. Then "'HALleLUjah.' ALmost" with its flip to trochees. Or compare second lines: "comPOser of choRALES," "this MASterY which NONE," "UTmost ABsoLUtist." Set against the regular syllabic length is a highly varying accentual music: counterpoint. You can find such cross-purposes, such counterpoint, throughout the poem. Likewise you can find it throughout most of her poems. Syllable and accent argue; they fluctuate. Look how light the beats in "from MINiature THUNder" (two beats?) that rise and congeal—crescendo—into the very heavy, five-beat "LOVE'S SIGnaTURE ceMENting FAITH."

That "miniature thunder" line reminds me of one more aspect of Moore's syllabics. She was not exact. Most prosodists hold that, to be a form, syllabics must be precise. There's nothing keeping the form together other than the mere count of syllables, so if you get the count off-whack, it's just not syllabic. We tend to overlook Moore's exceptions and substitutions. But even that famous fish poem is imperfect in number. Look back some time and count. Syllabics was, I contend, as much or more for Moore a compositional method than an end-game goal. My point here is simple: the way Moore applies syllabic numbers and accentual beats provides a high irregularity, a dynamic counterpoint inside the music, measurement, and meaning of her work.

I mentioned earlier that the explorer's task is to map and to describe, to give shape and names to the newly discovered. Moore must count in the number of "first poets," to use Cary Nelson's good phrase—poets for whom it is still possible to envision and perhaps attain a kind of Edenic purity or primacy. Emerson called it "an original relation to the universe"; Whitman "barbaric." Nelson includes Roethke, Kinnell, Rich, and Merwin in the generation of "our last first poets," and now we are beyond them all, belated as Bloom says, posterior, posthumous even, writing without a view of the source, without an impulse to regain any paradise lost.

Marianne Moore's poems are sometimes like a trip through Eden, though Eden may have streetcars, libraries, and baseballs as well as pangolins, frigate pelicans, wood-weasels, peacocks, katydids, and angels. In a single poem, "An Octopus," we discover a whole strange world full of peculiar beings. One of her longest poems—and technically quite different from the tightly wrapped contrapuntal formalism of "Melchior Vulpius"—"An Octopus" is a poem of discursive rhetoric and an expansive free-verse structure. Here we find a fertile example of Moore's multiform language that prompts Grace Schulman to note that for "Marianne Moore, seeing an object meant speaking of its various aspects on many levels of discourse."

And what is this object in "An Octopus"? It is *not* an octopus, but rather a vast ice sheet, a frozen landscape we might initially assume to be lifeless and static. Yet the poem is a lush, precise, inclusive catalog of biota, all the flora and fauna, all the structure and environment to be encountered on these "twenty-eight ice-fields from fifty to five hundred feet thick." It is, in fact, Mt. Rainier, or the glacial field moving in inexorable slowness along the rock body of the mountain—a surprisingly dynamic place much like the tense, generative site in "The Fish," where the edge-effect of ocean and rocky shore provide a fertile ground for life.

The American explorer has historically turned Westward for inspiration and discovery. Patricia Willis notes Moore's own sojourn to Mt. Rainier—she calls it "Mount Tacoma" in the poem, using its native name—in July of 1922, when she spent two days on the mountain in a kind of Edenic (re)discovery. Willis adds that Paradise is even the name of the access point to Rainier's peak, a meadow "perched on the side of the great Nisqually Glacier." Moore attests to a self-conscious affiliation with the great Edenic namer, since the primary trope in her poem is the describing and naming of the many inhabitants of the present icy garden, thus enacting "such power as Adam had."

"An Octopus" with its 193 lines and two stanzas is an abundant catalog of details, a naturalist's cornucopia of living things from "miniature cavalcades of chlorophylless fungi" to "businessmen" and mountain guides. Again, part of the poem's irony derives from the richness of life Moore finds, and lists, on this supposedly barren landscape. She delights in them all: dozens of animals ("bears, elk, deer, wolves, goats, and ducks" as well as more a distinctive "nine-striped chipmunk / running with unmammal-like agility"); dozens of plants (heather-bells, avalanche lilies, spruce-twigs, alpine buckwheat); all manner of rocks and minerals (onyx, lava and pumice, gold and silver ore, "marble and jasper and agate / as if whole quarries had been dynamited"). Much of the movement of the poem consists of the accumulating specificity—and oddity—of these many diverse inhabitants.

As if to parallel the abundance and variform of the place's constituent parts, Moore's own language and diction vary widely, too, enacting an "original American menagerie of styles." She's having a great time, in a kind of linguistic pastiche, building up the "many levels of discourse" that Schulman noted, in layers, in verbal strata, like the tiered landscape of the glacier itself:

> "Like happy souls in Hell," enjoying mental difficulties, the Greeks
> amused themselves with delicate behavior
> because it was "so noble and so fair";
> not practiced in adapting their intelligence
> to eagle-traps and snow-shoes,
> to alpenstocks and other toys contrived by those
> "alive to the advantage of invigorating pleasures."

Here, in one of the poem's secondary arguments, Moore juxtaposes the rich originality and ingenuity—the intrepid push of exploration—of the American West with the "remote wisdom" of the classical Greeks. She criticizes the Greeks, who "like[d] smoothness" and who distrusted "what was back / of what could not be clearly seen." Moore prefers the "love of doing hard things" and those "[c]omplexities that still will be complexities / as long as the world lasts."

"An Octopus" is a poem of complex precision but also of delight, and in this way is rhetorically akin to the odic praise of "Melchior Vulpius." In her desire for "relentless accuracy" and "capacity for fact," Moore's additive rhetoric finds her turning everywhere for source material, and finding it. Nearly eighty of this poem's lines are given in quotation marks, as Moore pieces together her description from a wildly disparate range of sources. She quotes Henry James and Cardinal Newman, Muir and Ruskin, Sir William Bell (on bendable glass), London journalists, and American naturalists writing on the West. Amy Clampitt identifies a further humorous source: "Embedded in what at first appears to be no more than a sprawling catchall of quotations and descriptive details are a number of precepts drawn (as the poet's own notes disclose) from none other than the Rules and Regulations of the U.S. Department of the Interior!"

For Marianne Moore, to understand a thing, to make it poem-worthy, requires all of one's ingenuity and all available resources. It requires the "thing itself," to use Maureen McLane's phrase again, but also "the idea about the thing." That is, in "An Octopus," Moore identifies the rich variety of life on the vibrant glacier, the identities and behaviors of those things, but she also layers-in the living language—the quotations, histories, and citations which serve as "ideas" about those things. Rock formations, waterfalls, kittentails, and language itself, are equally biotic, and all part of the experience of enjoying the great glacier.

As her career developed, Moore became renowned for her skillful language, acclaimed for the energetic and enlivening power of her idiom and form. She so famously named things that David Wallace and Bob Young of Ford Motor Company, in 1955, invited her to submit "inspirational names" for the launch of the company's newly developed experimental E-car. As Wallace reasoned, "Who better to understand the nature of words than a poet?" Moore accepted the challenge. Here are some of her actual suggestions in reply to Ford's solicitation: The Anticipator, Thunder Crester, The Silver Sword, The Resilient Bullet, The Regina Racer, The Magigravue, The Turcotingo, The Pastelogram, The Varsity Stroke, The Mongoose Civique, The Intelligent Whale, The Adante Con Moto, and her last one, The Utopian Turtletop. These could be comic books titles or superheroes, symphonies or school cheers; they could easily be part of the peculiar flora and fauna growing on Mt. Rainier.

In fact, Ford Motor had designed quite a car, with its big bubble top and horseshoe-shaped grill. It was also a record-setting flop, a complete dud, though the first reviews have a kind of Moore-like poetry to them. One calls this car "an Oldsmobile sucking a lemon," while another says it looks like "a Pontiac pushing a toilet seat." From Mr. Wallace's final letter to Marianne Moore: "We have chosen a name. . . . It fails somewhat of the resonance, gaiety and zest we were seeking. But it has a personal dignity and meaning to many of us here. Our name, dear Miss Moore, is—Edsel." How's that for a rejection letter.

Marianne Moore's poems are a rich atlas of signs and wonders: maps, measurements, and metrical contours of the language's idiosyncratic flexibility, with a dense population of creatures and citizens, whom she calls by name and recognizes in detail and with a glee both exacting and generative. For such a humble point of view—no confessional spew in these poems, no autobiography on display—her poems brightly overflow with the personality of engagement, presence, and invention. They remain alive, to use Edward Taylor's words, with "the Shine of Shining things made fine."

Gwendolyn Brooks

ON RIOTING AND *RIOT*

Mundane and Plural: "Riot"

David Baker

Trauma tends to paralysis. The traumatized are struck, as in shock, into inaction in a posture of wordless gaping. After great pain, as we know, a formal feeling comes. The nerves sit ceremonious, like tombs. Or, as another theorist of disaster has written, Maurice Blanchot, "We feel that there cannot be any experience of the disaster, even if we were to understand disaster to be the ultimate experience. This is one of its features: it impoverishes all experience, withdraws from experience all authenticity; it keeps its vigil only when night watches without watching over anything." Blanchot knows firsthand what it is to die and become alive again. In his miniature, post-traumatic memoir of his own near-extermination by firing squad, *The Instant of My Death*, he tries to write that "feeling of extraordinary lightness . . . sovereign elation," when the guns were lowered and the squad "moved away." At this moment of doubleness—"Dead—immortal"—he realizes that he cannot "try to analyze." And then aftermath. Just so, the ecstatic dissolves. To be standing beside himself, or away from himself, out of himself, *ex stasis*, is also to be standing for himself merely. The result is both mundane and plural: "As if the death outside of him could only henceforth collide with the death in him."

An unarmed Missourian, Michael Brown, was indeed shot to death on August 9, 2014, in Ferguson, by a fellow Missourian and policeman, Darren Wilson. Mundane and plural. Please understand me: no individual death is mundane. Brown's death is tragic and criminal, like Walter Scott's—who was shot in the back eight times by a South Carolina policeman Michael Slager—and thus plural, many times over. The recurrent and persisting horror of police shootings of unarmed people, young people, people of color, young men, the history of our country's worst horror and abiding shame that ranges from castration to lynching, one-at-a-time brutality as well as civil war—all our uncivil wars—is so recurrent and persisting *as to appear mundane*. It is the unmatched horror of seeing and living with brutality long settled into horrible habit and sanctioned, as it were, by the state, by the very state of things. In Brown's case the resulting response ranged (past tense?) from outrage—on all sides—to riots to calls-for-action, even for poetry. Yet I could not then write a poem. I have, since, written specifically about Ferguson, but like many, I imagine, the trauma, and anger, and sorrow are also finding themselves articulated, as Dickinson said, at a slant.

What I did, on the night of the first riot, was not riot but read. I turned to two poems. Whitman's "When Lilacs Last in the Dooryard Bloom'd" and something by Gwendolyn Brooks I had read many years before and not since.

Riot by Gwendolyn Brooks is a poem and a book. A tiny book in three parts (the first part is the title poem), totaling fourteen pages of print. It is a work markedly different from Brooks's famous earlier works. It is not typically part of the Brooks canon —I mean those anthologizable, more easily teachable poems. "The Bean Eaters," "We Real Cool," the rich portraits and populated neighborhoods of Bronzeville with their old relatives and crazy women, their children of the poor, their gay chaps and "pooh-pooh[ing]" preachers, established her reputation so quickly that her second book, *Annie Allen*, in 1950 won the Pulitzer Prize. She was the first black poet (she preferred this designation to African American) to win this prize. Here are the opening lines of "Riot":

> John Cabot, out of Wilma, once a Wycliffe,
> all whitebluerose below his golden hair,
> wrapped richly in right linen and right wool,
> almost forgot his Jaguar and Lake Bluff;
> almost forgot Grandtully (which is The
> Best Thing That Ever Happened To Scotch); almost
> forgot the sculpture at the Richard Gray
> and Distelheim; the kidney pie at Maxim's,
> the Grenadine de Boeuf at Maison Henri.

Because the Negroes were coming down the street.

Because the Poor were sweaty and unpretty
(not like Two Dainty Negroes in Winnetka)
and they were coming toward him in rough ranks.
In seas. In windsweep. They were black and loud.
And not detainable. And not discreet.

What just happened here? Where are we? John Cabot? Who? Gone are many characteristics of Brooks's earlier work: a fairly overt exterior narrative and linear chronology; a fixed or stable speaker, an individual "persona" with a voice lifted out of a Chicago Southside neighborhood and into (as she said) a "small second-floor apartment at the corner." Gone are the distinct and distinctly drawn characters, the jazzy mood, the ballad and sermon and blues intonations of her earlier poems. What we have instead is an intense, interiorized, self-referential work that feels more fragmented than complete, more cubist, more elliptical, more postmodernist than finished or tidily coherent. Its references seem social though they are uncontextualized and unexplained; and it leads into the poem's second section whose primary "strength . . . is how it uses collage," to cite a colloquium from Jacket2. What just happened here, in fact, is a riot.

Martin Luther King authorizes the poem with his opening assertion-epigraph that "a riot is the language of the unheard." And though the poem does not confirm—rather it assumes this circumstance, as it assumes our complicity in knowing [and in fact we can't not know what we know]—the triggering event is King's assassination, on April 4, 1968, and the aftermath riots in Chicago, the West Side or "race riots" in a city infamous for race riots, including the 1919 riots which featured heavily militarized police and thirty-eight deaths. The poem begins in the aftershock of trauma and seems to describe the fear and apparently, or likely, the death of one John Cabot, he of the "golden hair."

A critic calls this a "revisionary . . . even aspirational, history." In reality, no white people died in the riots—all eleven people who died were black. So who is John Cabot? A fiction, a figment, a straw figure? We know the name from history books, if we look. John Cabot—Giovanni Caboto—under commission from Henry VII, explored swaths of this continent in 1497, claiming North America for England, one of the first colonial appropriations of the new world. And we know John Cabot, according to the Jacket2 colloquium, as the "name of an original Boston Brahmin, about whose family it is said *and this is good old Boston . . . where the Lowells talk only to Cabots, and the Cabots talk only to God.*" We know our John Cabot is indeed talking to God, or "any handy angel," praying in horror: "Don't let It touch me! the blackness! Lord!" He sees the "windsweep" of Negroes coming down the street. He is grossed out by them. But "gross gross" may describe his own appetite or obesity, too, his outsized hunger for kidney pie and Grenadine de Boeuf, as for the other opulent aspects of his lifestyle, perhaps faux-European: fancy cars, fine clothes, rarified Scotch whiskey (though Grandtully is actually a cheap after-dinner liqueur, as well as a Scottish village, pronounced *grantly*). As he lived, he seems—this sacrificial J. C.—to "die expensively today," burning like the body of another holy martyr, John Wycliffe:

> Gross. Gross. "*Que tu es grossier!*" John Cabot
> itched instantly beneath the nourished white
> that told his story of glory to the World.
> "Don't let It touch me! the blackness! Lord!" he whispered
> to any handy angel in the sky.
> But, in a thrilling announcement, on It drove
> and breathed on him: and touched him. In that breath
> the fume of pig foot, chitterling and cheap chili,
> malign, mocked John. And, in terrific touch, old
> averted doubt jerked forward decently,
> cried, "Cabot! John! You are a desperate man,
> and the desperate die expensively today."
>
> John Cabot went down in the smoke and fire
> and broken glass and blood, and he cried "Lord!
> Forgive these nigguhs that know not what they do."

Aftermath: The poem seems to embody a tactic Brooks herself deliciously called "verse journalism": "I've always thought of myself as a reporter." But then, again, who is John Cabot? Is he not fictive rather than real? Does Brooks not seem empowered increasingly to imagine as well as document? Throughout *Riot* her poetic grows ever more complex and multiple, as even here, in this first section, her point-of-view is a superimposition, one on another, shared, plural, blended, yet also capable of particularizing time, sympathy, culpability, and indictment.

Aftermath: "Riot," the sequence's first part, exists forcefully as an artful expression of chaos, the first coming-into-words utterance after a stunned stupor in the wake of assassination. Riot sounds like rage. But it exists with equal force and fixity as an expression of the poet's confidence, her profound risk-taking, as she grows and develops. It's not that Brooks is turning away from her earlier poetic self; rather, she is becoming her later self, more fierce yet also more elliptical. In 1967, she attended the second Fisk Black Writers' Conference. The first conference, held in 1966—during the aftermath of the Watts riots and the assassinations of Malcolm X and Medgar Evers—called for a new black writing, affiliated with the Black Arts Movement. In *Riot* we see Brooks helping to shape this aesthetic. As the Jacket2 critics put it, we also see her opting out of a number of mainstream or established conventions: her celebrated signature idiom, her finesse with traditional prosody and form. (If this first part of *Riot* is loose pentameter, or at least deca- and hendecasyllabic lines—like the King quote, in fact—the subsequent sections eschew such formalism, as Carl Phillips's following essay will examine.) Elizabeth Alexander says about Brooks's early work that she is "nothing short of a technical virtuoso" with an impressive formal range of "sonnets, ballads, spirituals, blues, full and off-rhymes." She also opts out of other aspects that made her famous. *Riot* is Brooks's first book after she decided to leave Harper & Row and invest, as it were, with a black publisher—in this case Broadside Press, which Dudley Randall founded in 1965 and ran out of his spare bedroom and, later, a church basement in Detroit. That is, Brooks shifts her own cultural capital from New York to the Midwest, from a white board of trustees to "community publishing," in a decision James Sullivan calls a "profoundly anti-economic move." It's one thing to write black, to "maketh a brand new Black," and a further one to say "I couldn't possibly think of going back to any white publisher. I'll always be with a black publisher."

It's true that Brooks later expressed some doubt about *Riot*. Perhaps it was, she said, too meditative. But what she calls meditative may be the powerful interiority of her new style. Certainly it is not serene, it is not self-contained or self-reflective, it is not in its mood or method contemplative. It is powerfully dramatic, performed by a shifting cast of voices and not a single monologist; it is powerfully narrative, though its narrative field is highly elliptical, inferential, and as fluid as a photographic multiple-exposure.

Aftermath: An unarmed citizen, Abraham Lincoln, was shot to death on April 14, 1865 (he died the next morning), in Washington D.C., by a fellow citizen, the famous actor John Wilkes Booth. The Civil War stands as a kind of sustained traumatizing riot, fought in the nation's own backyards and neighborhoods; and Walt Whitman's great poem, the lilac poem, stands as elegy not just for the martyred Lincoln, not just for the legions of sacrificed war dead, but for the ideal notion of perfectibility, democracy's promising dream of equality and fairness. It was a riot of race, economics, and power. To express his grief, but also to enact a sympathetic martyrdom, Whitman dies, too, in his poem, his unsurpassed eloquence erased by horror and disillusionment. The great poet of the people retreats to a dismal inhuman swamp, giving himself over to grief. "Dead—Immortal," says Blanchot. In this same double trope, Whitman is reborn in the song of the hermit thrush, who tutors him in nature's forgiving and regenerative process. It is, we appreciate, one of the great acts of transcendental imagination. I'm sure that's why I turned to it when the riots began. And why I turned to Brooks? If Whitman's poem is a masterpiece of transcendence, Brooks's is a masterpiece of something else entirely. She does not transcend, does not rise remade, reunified, or reinvented out of the erasures of history and nature; not for her the intimate or egotistical sublime. Computer scientists have a term, when they include one document (or let's say one point of view, or voice, or tactic) inside or alongside another one: transclusion. Not to go beyond, but to reach beyond to include the other, or other things: textual blending, reaching out of, to attain the multiple. To perform transclusion is to carry from one thing to another, to overlay—not to go beyond, but to remain, enlarged. So this is the claim I make for Gwendolyn Brooks's later art. It is a transclusive art.

For Whitman, the figure of Lincoln stood as a figurehead—the ideal representative man, to use Emerson's term—a leader born straight out of the natural environment of the new world. Martin Luther King holds a similar esteem and position here in Brooks's post-Romantic, post-naturalist vision. But for us, of course, Michael Brown is neither a heroic elected politician, a president, a revered leader of a church, nor the embodiment of a civil rights movement. He was and is, like us, more mundane; like us, plural. Yet in this way, he is also a representative man. Neither hero nor anti-hero. But now, like Walter Scott, like Freddie Gray, and so many more, one of many. Blanchot again is useful here. He reminds us: "This self is merely a formal necessity; [but it does serve] to allow the infinite relation of Self to Other."

I know this one thing for certain. No one of us now—no one stunned self or Self—can supply a sufficient vision, a sufficient artwork, capable of addressing, representing, and correcting the horror of inequity, inequality, and human violence. This was Whitman's realization, too, and it nearly killed him. It is what Kazim Ali points to when he writes: "When we think of a unified or singular American identity, we lose the chance to truly understand our selves and one another." The really traumatic question is both plural and mundane. That question is, together, do we stand a chance?

Brooks's Prosody: Three Sermons on the Warpland

Carl Phillips

As Gwendolyn Brooks famously said in her *Report from Part I*, "Until 1967 my own blackness did not confront me with a shrill spelling of itself"–1967 being when she attended the Second Black Writers' Conference at Fisk University. What she seems to have meant was that a different way of feeling, understanding, and *writing* blackness overcame her. For to be sure, her work prior to this is grounded in black family, speakers, and issues. But that work was also cast in sonnets, the iambic pentameter line of blank verse, the traditional English prosody—the master's tools, as I sometimes think of them (master, as in master and slave)—of which Brooks had shown herself to be a master, culminating in the Pulitzer for *Annie Allen*, a book that both acknowledges a debt to and deftly reworks another "white classic," Virgil's *Aeneid*. After Fisk, Brooks seems to have had a sort of crisis of prosodic consciousness; it's as if she has to rethink what it means to use English prosodic tradition, now that she has subscribed to the Black Arts Movement's imperative to speak specifically to a Black audience, in language shaped primarily by motivating content, and less in terms of stylistic virtuosity. It's not that her poems hadn't been readable by blacks, but her prosody, in a sense, made for a receptive white audience—made her 'palatable,' I want to say, even if in certain poems ("The Lovers of the Poor," for example), she was skewering a white elite's condescending attitude toward blacks. The challenge, for Brooks, was to come up with a poetry, and a prosody to go with it, that would speak not so much to a largely white academy as to the kinds of people she'd been documenting, the bean-eaters, Satin Legs Smith, and the Rangers, those gang members she'd begun working with in writing workshops in Chicago.

Many readers say that this is where Brooks's work goes into decline, suggesting that she abandoned her prosodic gifts even as she exchanged a high literary idiom for a decidedly more demotic one. It is interesting how evolution in one writer can win praise, and in another be disparaged. What I want to look at here is how, in her suite of three sermons on the Warpland, we can see Brooks finding a way to adapt, rather than sacrifice, her mastery of prosody to her new sense of blackness; and across the three sermons, we can see, as well, an enactment of Brooks's wrestling with, straddling, and ultimately reconciling the seeming conflict between English prosody and the language of Black revolution.

How to negotiate the inevitable braid of black and white in American history? "The Sermon on the Warpland" exemplifies that braid:

> And several strengths from drowsiness campaigned
> but spoke in Single Sermon on the warpland.
>
> And went about the warpland saying No.
> "My people, black and black, revile the River.
> Say that the River turns, and turn the River.
>
> Say that our Something in doublepod contains
> seeds for the coming hell and health together.
> Prepare to meet
> (sisters, brothers) the brash and terrible weather;
> the pains;
> the bruising; the collapse of bestials, idols.
> But then oh then!—the stuffing of the hulls!
> the seasoning of the perilously sweet!
> the heath! the heralding of the clear obscure!"

At the most obvious level, you can hear how, for the first three stanzas, each line is a pentameter line–mostly iambic–with the obvious exceptions of the foreshortened lines 8 and 10. So, in the tradition of Claude McKay's "Harlem Dancer," Cullen's "Yet Do I Marvel" and, contemporary with Brooks herself, Robert Hayden's "Middle Passage,"—and consistent with all of her work pre-Fisk—Brooks here, at the level of meter, uses English—white—prosody for black purposes, shaping the master's language to her own subject matter, a decidedly non-white one. What I'm more interested in, though, is the rhyme scheme that governs these first three stanzas, one that unites these fourteen lines into a stylized sonnet. As you can see, we open with a rhyming couplet. Line three is the only line that finds no rhyme, deliberately, I'd say; the line itself ends with the word "No"—it seems appropriate that the imperative to resist "Yes" should resist rhyme's closure. This is followed by the exact rhyme of "River" and "River." But look at what happens after this: an interlocking set of rhymes which create no fewer than four instances of sonic chiasmus. ABBA, CDDC, BDDB, and BCCB:

Contains	A
Together	B
Meet	C
Weather	B
Pains	A
Idols	D
Hulls	D
Sweet	C
Obscure	B

Cage within a cage within a cage, we might say – or frame within a frame within a frame. Chiasmus as a rhetorical device tends to suggest sometimes the comfort of containment, other times the claustrophobia of captivity. Brooks seems to be using chiasmus here not to answer but to provoke questions. How far is captivity from containment? What's the difference between comfort and complacency, between claustrophobia and incipient rage? After which, she abandons the sonnet, and this seems to trigger anaphora (anaphora an element of oratory as long ago as Thucydides and Cicero, but also a prominent device in the oratory of the black church).

> "Build now your Church, my brothers, sisters. Build
> never with brick nor Corten nor with granite.
> Build with lithe love. With love like lion-eyes.
> With love like morningrise.
> With love like black, our black –
> luminously indiscreet;
> complete; continuous."

We've seen it earlier in this poem, but here it governs the stanza, three sentences opening with "Build," three with "With love like," in a stanza of fairly steadily diminishing lines, metrically speaking: 3 pentameter, 2 trimeter, 1 tetrameter, and then a 2-beat dimeter finale. But Brooks holds onto chiasmus. One straddles stanzas 3 and 4: "(sisters, brothers)" at line 9 and "brothers, sisters" at 15; and then, as if for final reinforcement, the last two lines have a chiasmus of rhyme:

luminously indiscreet;	A	B
complete, continuous	B	A

What to make of a cage, if cage it be, that sounds so lovely? Or is this the X—the chi of chiasmus—by which those who cannot sign otherwise leave their mark?

"The Sermon on the Warpland" shows Brooks using English prosody as a vehicle for exhorting a black audience to say no, to "Prepare to meet . . . the pains" that will come with resisting the reviled River. In part, the combination of that form and content embody the intertwinedness of blacks and whites, even as the poem's final stanza suggests a departure from English prosody to one that we more associate with black culture. "The Second Sermon on the Warpland" strikes me as the enacting of a more complete departure. No ghost of a sonnet here, in this poem of four sections of widely varying length. Brooks is direct about this in section two, announcing (in a pentameter line) that "not the pet bird of poets, that sweetest sonnet,/shall straddle the whirlwind." Rhyme all but falls away. Chiasmus is absent—no cage, no comfort here. Also gone is any sustained pentameter—where it appears, it gets quickly undercut by foreshortened lines. In section three, lines 2-5 are pentameter, but all three open with a reversed foot (a revolt from the iamb?) and two of them are on the baggy side because of some anapests in the mix. The shift from these lines to the three that follow feels like stepping into a space that's quieter and more clear—it feels like freedom, a freedom linked to the absence of predictable sonic pattern:

> All about are the cold places,
> all about are the pushmen and jeopardy, theft –
> all about are the stormers, and scramblers but
> what must our Season be, which starts from Fear?
> Live and go out.
> Define and
> medicate the whirlwind.

Restraint, and release, played out in such a way as to suggest not just prosodic restlessness but the restlessness of an entire people. And—or?—it also seems as if Brooks is arguing for a kind of equality at the level of prosody and, by extension, the level of human lives. Hence lines like "cracks into furious flower. Lifts its face / all unashamed. And sways in wicked grace . . ."—pentameter and rhymed—are on equal footing with lines like

> A garbageman is dignified
> as any diplomat.
> Big Bessie's feet hurt like nobody's business.

This is less a dismantling of English prosody than a rejection of its supremacy. There will have to be room made, the *prosody* tells us, for otherness, and on an equal footing. Not the least part of the prosody, here, is how all four sections are yoked together by the words "live" and "the whirlwind" at the end of each section, as if the relationship between the whirlwind of racial oppression and the need to live in the face of it were not just the one unavoidable fact, but strangely, an organizing principle – for the poem, yes, but also, implicitly, for the kind of communal energy required if resistance to injustice is to effect any real change.

"The Third Sermon on the Warpland" is actually part of a sequence, "Riot," but Brooks's title suggests that we are to read this with an understanding of there having been two earlier sermons—hence, my consideration of the three together. "The Third Sermon" does stand apart, though, in not being governed by the imperative, there's no sense of an addressee. Rather, this sermon unfolds by exposition, a filmic narrative of a riot that has broken out, less exhortation, more notational in style, many of the lines are of overheard dialogue in a crowd, some read like stage directions in drama. The English pentameter that figured prominently in the first sermon, then seemed intertwined with demotic speech in the second, here becomes the minority; more often than not, what pentameter there is seems incidental, as it is in conversation. This seems fitting in a poem in which two philosophers, whom Brooks calls simply The Black Philosopher and The White Philosopher, seem to be in their own conversation as they get quoted across the poem—the Black Philosopher suggesting the violence to come as a result of white complacency, the White Philosopher pressing for hope in a time of despair, even as hope becomes force, hope manifested as black violence.

So, black rioting against white oppression = the eradication of English/white prosody, each an enactment of the other? Not quite. While Brooks has systematically pared away the traditional prosodic elements in the course of her three sermons, having cast aside the sonnet as irrelevant to social change in the second sermon, it seems she can't—won't—let go entirely. Near the end of the third sermon, I detect a sonnet. Not the single fourteen-line stanza of the poem that serves as an elegy for a dead woman – yes, it's 14 lines, but not enough of the other elements to convince me it's a sonnet. I mean the one 15-line stanza, whose first line announces itself as the title, "A Poem to Peanut," in which Brooks presents a portrait of the Rangermen as the new heroes.

A Poem to Peanut.	
"Coooooool!" purrs Peanut. Peanut is	
Richard – a Ranger and a gentleman.	A
A Signature. A Herald. And a Span.	A
This Peanut will not let his men explode.	
And Rico will not.	
Neither will Sengali.	
Nor Bop nor Jeff, Geronimo nor Lover.	B
These merely peer and purr,	C
and pass the Passion over.	B
The Disciples stir	C
And thousandfold confer	C
with ranging Rangermen;	A
mutual in their "Yeah!—	D
this AIN'T all upinheah!"	D

You can see that the poem is almost entirely iambic. Four of the lines are iambic pentameter, and five of the last six lines are trimeter. Meanwhile, there's a rhyme scheme of sorts, one that offers us a Shakespearean quatrain, as well as a rhyming couplet for an ending. The BCBCCA of lines 7-12 aren't exactly the sestet of a Petrarchan sonnet, but they suggest something of the same patterning of resolution that the sestet offers, even as the A rhyme of "Rangermen" ties the poem's latter half to the words "gentleman" and "span" at the poem's beginning. I think Brooks wants us to think of the sonnet, as she wants us to think of heroic tradition—differently. Through the lens of blackness as activism, not as presentation piece. My sense is she stood somewhere between Malcolm X and Martin Luther King, Jr., in terms of her sensibility. She recognizes the usefulness of violence, the necessity for it—but she also somewhere believes, to quote the third sermon's opening line, that "The earth is a beautiful place"—she won't have it destroyed. Likewise she won't abandon the traditional English prosody that she so clearly loves. But she seems to have seen its limitations, if not made to adapt to cultural change.

Most things revolutionary aren't so much about newness as about understanding the past enough to know what to save of it, and to shape the rest into what, in effect, can bring the old forward to renewed relevance. From the evidence of her three sermons on the warpland, this is the achievement of Brooks after Fisk. Hardly a decline. Rather she manages to move forward, her gifts intact but newly relevant, deployed in the service of a racial climate vastly different from where she first began.

The Eros in Democracy: "An Aspect of Love, in Ice and Fire"

Meghan O'Rourke

Why does a book-length poem called "Riot" (1969), which details the civic unrest in 1968 Chicago after Martin Luther King Jr.'s assassination, conclude with not a bang, as it were, but with an intimate domestic scene between two lovers? What accounts for this private, interior, semi-erotic tableaux? Encountering it in an anthology, you might think this poem reads almost like a traditional love lyric. Most political poetry does not—imagine, say, Shelley's "The Masque of Anarchy" ending with a bedroom scene. It's much easier to imagine a version of "Riot" that ends with a hortatory, impersonal from-on-high vision of renewal, something like Auden's "we must love one another / or die" or Audre Lorde's "The difference between poetry and rhetoric / is being ready to kill / yourself / instead of your children." In fact, when "Riot" was anthologized in the Library of America's *The Essential Gwendolyn Brooks*, this third section was left out, presumably because the editors considered it less important than the first two sections, which are, on a superficial read, more overtly "political." But what I want to argue here is that in some sense the real politics of this poem lie with its ending—that you cannot omit the ending without neutering or, in some sense, whitewashing Brooks's vision. In some ways this poem is *more* political and original because of this tiny lyric.

The third part of "Riot" is the shortest of the three sections, taking up little more than a page. It comprises seven stanzas, several of which are one line:

It is the morning of our love.

In a package of minutes there is this We.
How beautiful.

Merry foreigners in our morning,
we laugh, we touch each other,
are responsible props and posts.

A physical light is in the room.

Because the world is at the window
we cannot wonder very long.

You rise. Although
genial, you are in yourself again.
I observe
Your direct and respectable stride.
You are direct and self-accepting as a lion
In African velvet. You are level, lean,
remote.

There is a moment in Camaraderie
when interruption is not to be understood.
This is the shining joy;
the time of not-to-end.

On the street we smile.
We go
in different directions
down the imperturbable street.

Because this section is quite different from the first two sections of the poem, which are polyvocal, fragmentary, and overtly sociopolitical in nature, to read "Riot" is to have to ask why it ends with an invocation of individual and—crucially—*erotic* renewal.

There are two interconnected answers. For one thing, Brooks wanted, I think, to push back against the popular white vision of an "undifferentiated mass" of rioters. (See, for example, the lines in section one when the rioters are seen by the white John Cabot: "the Negroes were coming down the street… / they were coming toward him in rough ranks. . . . / They were black and loud. / And not detainable.") It is implied that the lovers are black, and it would seem, then, that she wanted to write a political poem that concluded with an indelible portrait of black people as individuals—in this case, as giddy, optimistic lovers, not as "types" or "rough ranks." But I also would argue, as importantly, that she wanted to reinscribe a Whitmanic vision of democratic ideals in terms of the political goals reflected in the Black Arts Movement—to ring a change on the dominant poetic vision of American democracy. What I am suggesting is that this poem's evocation of two people going to bed together, rising, and then walking down a street "in different directions" is for Brooks a model of the possibilities of an egalitarian society. In her view, to model that society one has to begin, as Whitman did, with the tender connection between two people. In her book *Renegade Poetics: Black Aesthetics and Formal Innovation in African American Poetry*, the critic and poet Evie Shockley has described one aspect of Brooks's work as a kind of "changing the subject," and that is, I think, an apt way of describing what she does here.

But first let's look at the poem. "Riot" has been relatively neglected within Brooks's canon, mainly because its political subversiveness led some critics to dismiss it. Because this section in particular has received little attention, I want to offer a close reading of it—after all, part of my argument is simply that this work as a whole merits close critical scrutiny of the sort that it largely did not receive, and that this section is crucial to understanding the whole work. I would like, too, to complicate the cut-and-dried, pre- and post-1967 narrative about Brooks's prosody—a line I know Brooks herself drew, and which Carl Phillips has written here about—by noting how much this piece of the poem is still influenced by Brooks's erstwhile modernism, in particular by T. S. Eliot. To my ear "The Waste Land" is a shadow text behind "Riot." There are the surface allusions and overlaps: the title of the second part ("The Third Sermon," like "The Fire Sermon"; the reliance on "Fire" as a destructive and renewing element). There is the sonic overlay of "waste land" and "warp land." And there are the textual resonances: the use of capitalized words spoken by some external, unidentified voice; the disjunctiveness of the prosody; the difficulty we find in locating a central speaker; the alternation of longer and shorter lines. America, Brooks implies, is a kind of Waste Land following King's death, not because the unrest is unjustified—indeed, the poem appears to suggest that, given American history, riot is a legitimate avenue for political reform. Rather, it's a Waste Land because of the very injustice and oppression that led to the riots. But for Brooks, writing about revolution does not mean eschewing entirely the techniques and influences of the poets whose work informed her as a young poet.

This section is different from the two that precede it. It is not strictly speaking polyvocal, fragmentary, or highly elliptical in its treatment of its subject. Tender in tone, the poem paints a vivid picture of two lovers in a room, getting ready to leave it. Maybe they've just woken; certainly they're just getting out of bed. There is a distinct first-person speaker, speaking to a "you" who appears to be a new lover. But, it's worth noting, for most of the poem, Brooks uses first person plural pronouns ("we" and "our"), emphasizing the *couple* and its unity. A few of the lines—including the first—are in an iambic tetrameter, and many others are in something close to it. So a kind of shadowy order is always about to come into focus beneath the free-verse rhythm. (Partly it's this that brings Eliot to mind: many of his poems play with iambic tetrameter or a four-beat line.) The central action of the poem happens about halfway through:

> You rise. Although
> genial, you are in yourself again.

These lines—to state the obvious—suggest a literal rising from bed following the entanglement and self-forgetfulness of sex. With rising comes a reassuming of individuality and separateness; in fact, the lines are a very beautiful description of an almost universal moment. Given the broader context of the poem, though, we also have to take the verb "rise" here in its metaphorical guise: "you rise" is also evocative of a post-riot social renewal of blacks in

America, a vision of what is happening on the streets of Chicago.

This gesture, the crux of the poem, stages the poem's subsequent shift from erotic entanglement to a clear—and arresting—view of the other as other. The speaker suddenly sees the "you" as a distinct human with his or her own intentions and physical qualities, and, implicitly, needs and rights. In fact, the next two descriptive lines are unlike anything else in the poem: they slow the poem down and almost seem unnecessary, until one realizes that they crucially enact and *embody* the act of witnessing the other. The speaker doesn't just acknowledge the lover, but bears meaningful testimony to his irreducible being:

> I observe
> your direct and respectable stride.
> You are direct and self-accepting as a lion
> in Afrikan velvet. You are level, lean,
> remote.

The adjectives are worth pausing over—"direct," "respectable," "self-accepting," "Afrikan." Nearly all (except "Afrikan") are explicitly qualitative. Note, too, that this is the one place in the poem the "We" breaks down into "you" and "I." Here, Brooks is consciously reinscribing agency and personhood to the lover, rejecting the kinds of reductive, racist narratives white society has traditionally imposed on him or her. In their place, she introduces a fresh, new, particularized, vocabulary of recognition.

The other significant action at the poem comes at the end:

>   we go
> in different directions
> down the imperturbable street.

Here we find an example of Brooks's double vision—the way she is trying to capture a sensation of both connection and separation, a quality David Baker calls the "double duty" of her work. The lovers, still giddy from a night of "wonder," walk freely "in different directions." On the one hand, this is a literal description of a couple parting. On the other, on a deeper level, the description is a kind of completion of the individualization we saw earlier: having been connected, giddy and hopeful in the "morning of their love," they must part, moving into their regular days. They are at once plural and singular.

That word "imperturbable" is worth pausing over, as it does a huge amount of work in the poem. It means "not to be confused or disturbed." The jacket copy on the back of *Riot* tellingly describes the riots as "disturbances." So within the materialist presentation of the work—Brooks had input, as far as I understand, on how this edition was made, working closely with Broadside Press and with Dudley Randall—"imperturbable" is a countervision, a counterhistory. It evokes an *undisturbed* street or a street where riots are no longer necessary. On such a street, the lovers can part and move on into their lives. It is a vision of a future democratic society: a social space of calm.

But I suspect there is something else going on here too. Around the time of the publication of "Riot," Brooks found herself in the position of being criticized from both sides. Conservative white critics had criticized her for abandoning her "traditional" forms–the tightly made sonnets and persona poems we saw in *A Street in Bronzeville* and other books. But some in the Black Arts Movement thought her work was not radical enough. She was older than many of the younger members, and her earlier body of work suggested an uncritical participation in a hierarchical white literary world. Some, like Haki Madhubuti, saw her work's connection to modernism as a kind of capitulation to white values, an abandonment of black identity and its aesthetics. And so one might read the end as an expression of Brooks's hope that within the African-American community there could be a unified understanding that renewal might go hand-in-hand with people going in different directions—i.e., that there would be different (and perhaps equally valid) visions of what change ought to look like. Notably, "In different directions" was sufficiently important a phrase that it was used as the title for a 1975 selection of her poems in the Library of Congress's *Quarterly Journal*—presumably chosen by her, or at least with her approval.

Clearly Brooks found it necessary to shift her focus to individual intimacy in order to conclude this big poem about social equality and social revolution. To me, there is a connection here, conscious or not, with Walt Whitman, another of our great political poets. In fact, it seems to me that in many ways this poem makes an implicit and important response to, and corrective of, Whitman. Whitman's poetry had at its heart a vision of democracy that depended on the eros between two individual members. "Song of Myself," it is worth remembering, was written partly in response to the deep racial divisions in America in the years before the Civil War; in it, Whitman articulates a vision of democratic unity grounded in erotic love between people (and across time).

As Whitman stages it, erotic love is the glue that binds democracies—a model for democratic feeling, a kind of erotic pluralism. What democracy demands of us, the philosopher Martha Nussbaum argues in *Political Emotions: Why Love Matter for Justice*, is that our feeling for our fellow citizens is stronger than our distrust or suspicion. And one way that happens, she argues, is through love and sympathetic identification that expand our "circle of concern." "All decent societies need to guard against division and hierarchy by cultivating appropriate sentiments of sympathy and love," she writes; her thesis is that art is one of the primary ways a liberal society achieves such sentiments. We rely on powerful works of art to jolt us out of the divisive feelings that, as she puts it, "inhibit our dealings with one another." Whitman's visionary poetry, in her view, is an example of one such artifact. Of his famous elegy for Abraham Lincoln, "When Lilacs Last in the Dooryard Bloom'd," she writes, "Participating emotionally in Whitman's poem, readers are summoned to throw their full hearts into the search for an America that does not yet exist, but which might become reality."

This insight—that a kind of eros of identification might enlarge us—was of course central to Whitman's work, and to his project of radical identification with the other. Likewise, in Brooks's poem, as in Whitman's, equality is driven by a kind of *caritas*/love that must be figured in the intimacy of the body if it is to succeed as a powerful symbol for the broader group. But there is a major difference between the two poems. Crucially, while the first two sections of Brooks's poem feature white people who don't get it, so to speak—"But WHY do these people offend themselves?" One says in Section Two—this section includes no white people (or none that we know of). In this way "Riot" participates in the Black Arts Movement's aesthetic attempt to construct a way of talking about black people and black life that didn't have to include or deal with white people, that didn't need white people to be part of the discourse. The vision in this section is inclusive of blacks but in some sense indifferent to or even exclusive of whites.

In offering this as its culminating democratic vision, "Riot" enacts a kind of "changing the subject," to borrow again from Shockley's characterization of what Brooks excelled at. If Whitman, as a white man in 1855, was saying, "Look, we are equal, you are like me," when he wrote to the African-American reader, Brooks, as a black woman in 1968, is saying to the white reader, "Look, we are equal, so much so that I don't even have to include you in my portrait of an egalitarian world–that is how far we have come." In this way, the end of "Riot" enacts change even as it envisions it. It concludes with a vision of democracy that, unlike Whitman's radical universalism ("And what I assume / you shall assume / For every atom belonging to me as good belongs to you"), is primarily pluralistic, reinforcing the idea of important differences among the larger group. All may have equal value, but they walk "in different directions"—an image quite different in affect than Whitman's image of atoms commingling.

It's something of a critical truism that the United States has a particularly impoverished tradition of politically engaged literature. It's also something of a critical truism—or at least an oft-invoked quandary—that, as W. H. Auden put it, in his elegy for the poet W. B. Yeats, "poetry makes nothing happen." But *Riot,* like Claudia Rankine's *Citizen: An American Lyric* reminds us of precisely what poetry can do that is different from prose. That is, poetry is able not only to articulate a vision, but to embody it. Poetry works on the limbic system, through the lyric qualities of music. This tradition of American embodiment is crucially somatic and ultimately hopeful in the way it crosses bridges and gives voice to the traumas of the culture at large and of people in particular.

Brooks's poem ends with a vision of an "imperturbable" street. As we know, that street is not yet here. And so her challenge remains one we have to take seriously. *Riot,* like much of Brooks's earlier work, about the violent history of white lynching, demands the reader ask what she might be blind to: What can I not see or what am I missing? What does a vision of pluralism mean, and how might we walk someday, in different directions, along an imperturbable street?

There is an idea in medicine of the illness that one is blind to or in denial about—"anosognosia," the illness that one has to be told one has. It is an illness so embedded in your subjectivity that it seems normal to you. Of course, it strikes one upon hearing this term that a culture too could suffer from "anosognosia." *Riot* succeeds, to a surprising degree, in forcing the reader to confront her own possible blindness—to confront the social ills she is complicit in, the ways a society can accept deep wrongs as "normal" without consciously intending to do so. What hasn't been fully understood, though, is how this tender, modernist-influenced, and strangely intimate last section of "Riot" is crucial to the poem's achievement.

W. S. Merwin

WORDS ON A JOURNEY

Erasure, Extinction, and the Work of Preservation

David Baker

When W. H. Auden selected *A Mask for Janus*, in 1951, for the Yale Series for Younger Poets award, he noted in his introduction the "admirable respect for [the] traditions of poetic craftsmanship" this new poet, W. S. Merwin, enacted. Auden was no slouch. His first Yale choice, in 1946, was Joan Murray's *Poems*, and before he finished his stint in 1958 with William Dickey's *Of the Festivity*, he had shown the series' most visionary selecting, picking such manuscripts as *A Change of World, The Green Wall, Some Trees, A Crackling of Thorns*. These are, you may recognize, the first books of Adrienne Rich, James Wright, John Ashbery, and John Hollander. Did you know that twice (three times, according to one source) Auden passed over a manuscript from one Sylvia Plath?

W. S. Merwin was twenty-four when *A Mask for Janus* appeared in 1952. (Plath, by the way, was nineteen.) Twenty-four, yet his work shimmered with the burnish of poetic formalism and the high literary tradition. He'd taken his degree as a scholarship student at Princeton, where he studied with the great critic, R. P. Blackmur, and roomed with Galway Kinnell. Can you imagine? Auden wrote at length about Merwin's application of myth, and praised his finesse with such forms as the Spanish carol. Auden finished off his introduction with a passage from de Toqueville, on destiny: "The destinies of mankind—man himself . . . standing in the presence of Nature and of God, with his passions, his doubts, his rare prosperities, and inconceivable wretchedness—will become the chief . . . theme of poetry." More about destiny shortly.

It's commonplace to find in Merwin's work the demonstration of a powerful poetic in his books from the 1960s and early 70s, his "second four books." There's no doubt of the surprise, the achieved and shocking originality of this work. It's pretty amazing: to have begun with such acquiescence to the tradition, or perhaps such thorough apprenticeship, and to have arrived at *The Lice*, in 1967, with such masterful dissatisfaction or rejection of that tradition. Isn't that eerily true of much of Merwin's great generation? The early books of Wright and Rich, of Bly, Kinnell, just earlier of Brooks, writing their sonnets, sestinas, and blank-verse ballads, sound also like juvenile Georgian poets, obeying their immediate fathers Ransom, Wheelock, I. A. Richards. Can you think of a generation who made such drastic metamorphoses?

So, my first of three points in this consideration. Merwin's work of the 1960s is a purposeful casting aside of his own academic, traditionalist poetry. Step by step he unwrites himself. He erases the inscriptions of self and the learned style of his young generation. Consider the opening quatrains of "Song," the final poem in *A Mask for Janus*, with its archaic diction and syntax, its rhymed couplets and dutiful tetrameter:

> Mirrors we lay wherein desire
> Traded, by dark, conceits of fire;
> As gardened minds whose delicacy
> Could neither close with flesh nor flee,
>
> Who watched by fire a bush inflect
> What flame a window could reflect
> Where dark and distance were control
> So the leaves burned yet rested whole. . . .

And now, from *The Moving Target* in 1963, this final poem, "Daybreak":

> Again this procession of the speechless
> Bringing me their words
> The future woke me with its silence
> I join the procession
> An open doorway
> Speaks for me
> Again

I'll say more about these changes shortly. But first a quick observation about developments *within* those first four books, changes harder to detect than the phoenix-like burst of new style—the deep image, the primitivist line, the naked word—that we find in his poems of the 60s. In those first four books, published in a flurry from 1952 to 1960, Merwin seems to maintain a stiff academic obedience. But style and subject matter are already morphing, from the heightened familiar mythologies in *A Mask for Janus* and *The Dancing Bears*, to, in *Green with Beasts* and especially *The Drunk in the Furnace*, a less arch formalism, disencumbered syntax, hints of a plainer diction, and subjects that include now sea tales, family portraits, and nature narratives. These are the foundational first steps of a quickening revisionism. You might see a less obvious casting off of gestural rhetoric. You might detect beginnings of a personal voice or story, though he was (and remains) far from the confessional revelations of those poets a decade older, like Lowell and Berryman, or the younger Plath.

I mean to assert that from the beginning Merwin enacts a purposeful erasure of tactic and gesture, shifting away from the monolithic mythology of Western literary traditionalism: an absenting or erasing of presence, even of aspects of history. Even in that first book, he writes in a beautiful passage at the end of "Dictum: For a Masque of Deluge," after seventy lines of stiff well-schooled impersonality, after a heavy allegorical retelling of the Flood myth, these lines:

> A falling frond may seem all trees. If so
> We know the tone of falling. We shall find
> Dictions for rising, words for departure;
> And time will be sufficient . . .
> To teach an order and rehearse the days
> Till the days are accomplished. . . .

It's a moment of near prophecy, speaking now in future tense, hoping to create an ideal "diction for rising" in order to discover "words for departure." These will be fundamental tropes in the coming great work.

And that great work arrives in 1963 with *The Moving Target* and extends through *The Lice, The Carrier of Ladders, Writings to an Unfinished Accompaniment* to *The Compass Flower* in 1977. I will resist a point-by-point look at Merwin's achievements in these incredible fourteen years, though I must say I find these books of such accomplishment that they stand, to me, as the great poetry of our language in our time. In fact, within a single book, *The Moving Target,* written in about three years, we see his development virtually *from one poem to the next,* letting go of more, in Merwin's art of absence and erasure.

The Moving Target consists of sixty-four poems arranged, roughly, in their order of composition. What evolves? A gradual erasure of capitalization and removal of punctuation (except white space), a radical loosening of the line, its regularity; but more deeply, a growing resistance to scholarly troping, dense conceits, and the archaic reiterations of familiar mythologies: a rebuttal of the formal markers of the era's poetry. He is unwriting, and when he commences his next book, *The Lice,* his mature style has fully arrived. As Laurence Lieberman famously announced, "If there is any book today that has perfectly captured the peculiar spiritual agony of our time . . . and has transformed that agony into great art, it is W. S. Merwin's *The Lice.*"

This is the moment of the birth of the contemporary deep image, the reversion to a primordial and primitivist poetic where "every memory is abandoned" ("The Finding of Reasons"). What is happening? Kinnell, Bly, and Wright are translating *duende* into English. Richard Howard is revealing the inventions of Roland Barthes and the French post-structuralists. Merwin is translating everything, as Ezra Pound advised the young Merwin to do, from Antonio Porchia and the essential (and essentialist) Jean Follain to all those proto-poetic "Asian figures," as he calls them. It's a purposeful meltdown of the firmament, not only in poetry, but culturally in its resistance to the war in Asia and the oppressions of a racist, materialist, misogynist zeitgeist. It's the birth of a new age in the death of the old regime.

"Poetry is the orphan of silence," writes Charles Simic in *The*

New Naked Poetry, calling for a "devastating simplicity": "There is a need here, an obsession with purity. . . . In the end I am always at the beginning. Poverty—an endless condition." Kinnell, in the same book, asserts that "the subject of the poem is the thing which dies. . . . Poetry is the wasted breath." And Merwin himself: "To recur in its purest forms . . . poetry seems to have to keep reverting to its naked condition, where it touches on all that is unrealized." The naked condition describes the new poem's stylistic aspirations, as well as its resistance of allegorical myth. Merwin activates this trope often in *The Carrier of Ladders*, as in his poem "Envoy from D'Aubigne":

> Go without ornament
> without showy garment
> if there is in you any
> joy
> may the good find it
>
> for the others be
> a glass broken in their mouths

My second point is that in rejecting the old literary style and mythology, erasure becomes not just a tactic, like a mere workshop prompt, but a trope. It becomes not just a means but a subject and a surrogate storyline. "We hurtle forward and seem to rise," he announces in the first lines of "Plane," the first poem in *The Carrier of Ladders*: "I imagine the deities come and go / without departures." Figure by figure, then, Merwin's task is concurrently to displace the old mythologies, dispatching them as departures, and to propose ingredients of a new mythos. One way to read these poems is to see them as identifications of the population—the aspects, the very atomic structure—of this new narrative. "Here is the air," he writes: "Nothing but me is moving / on these bridges / as I always knew it would be" ("The Bridges"). He maps the ghost world behind, within, beyond the known, as in "Beginning of the Plains": "wind without flags / marching into the city / to the rear."

He seeks his bearings as he narrates his eerie explorations:

> All through the dark the wind looks
> for the grief it belongs to
> ("Night Wind")

—and nominates what he finds on his journey:

> I recognize the first hunger
> as the plains start
> under my feet
> ("Beginning of the Plains")

Primacy, originality, a hunger for firstness is an essential paradox in Merwin's art; for it is an originality of after-effect, belated in history and yet intentional in its quest to replace that very history and its failed narratives. Did Merwin and the other deep-imagists essentially invent deconstruction before the deconstructions did their work?

> Now it is clear to me that no leaves are mine
> no roots are mine
> and wherever I go I will be a spine of smoke in the forest . . .
>
> and that the birds vanish because of something
> that I remember . . .
>
> it is clear to me that I cannot return
> but that some of us will meet once more
> even here
> like our own statues
> and some of us still later without names
> and some of us will burn with the speed
> of endless departures
> and be found and lost no more
> ("Now It Is Clear")

This new myth is a myth of negation, the *via negativa* both of mysticism and political resistance: "Maybe he does not even have to exist / to exist in departures / then the first darkness falls" ("The First Darkness").

Roethke agrees: "In a dark time the eye begins to see." So Merwin, after "the first darkness falls," sets out to repopulate like a shadow Adam the new world, even though "the eyes are not yet made that can see it." It's a moment of profound creation and origination: "the first composer / could hear only what we could write" ("Memory of Spring"). A moment of re-vision and endless definition:

> An hour comes
> To close a door behind me
> ("Memory of the Loss of Wings")

> As on each journey there is
> a silence that goes with it
> ("On Each Journey")

And its procedures are constructed as much by *what is not* as by what is:

> something I've not done
> is following me
> I haven't done it again and again
> ("Something I've Not Done")

> if it's invented it will be used
> maybe not for some time
> ("Tool")

This is a place where a door might be
here where I am standing
in the light outside all the walls . . .

and somebody would come and knock
on this air
long after I have gone
and there in front of me a life
would open
("A Door")

This is a vision made of such provisionals; a visionary culture made of absence and erasure, among shadows of the lost whose footsteps are semiotic traces pointing at once forward and backward into a void. It's a method made of mysticism as well as archetypes of the deep psyche. That is to say, if Merwin's achievement during this great period is the invention and imposition of a new mythology, it must be, in Anthony Libby's delicious phrase, a "mythology of nothing."

In the mid-1970s Merwin moved to an acreage on Maui, where he still lives, and from here his work has taken a further step, a third major development. So my final point proposes a final paradox: is it possible to see *all* of Merwin's work, the accumulated poetics of erasure and absence, as an act of preservation? After *Opening the Palm* (1983) and *The Rain in the Trees* (1988) his poetry takes on the specific task of natural custody and environmentalism, as his life's work as gardener and cultivator has deepened. Now the Merwin Conservancy is the product of his work to preserve the endangered palms. Now he explores Hawaiian epics, lost populations of trees, carrier pigeons, the endangered species from insects ("we kill you again and again") to humans, who are still alive even as we "[depart] from ourselves" ("Elders"). In the powerful volume *The Vixen,* from 1996, the fox serves as figure for the belated and departed, the elegized environment:

Comet of stillness princess of what is over
high held note without trembling without voice without sound

aura of complete darkness keeper of the kept secrets
  of the destroyed stories the escaped dreams the sentences
never caught in words

. . .

let me catch sight of you again going over the wall
  and before the garden is extinct and the woods are figures
guttering on a screen let my words find their own
  places in the silence after the animals
("Vixen")

In fact, if we look at his recent work, but also back to all his work, it's possible to retranslate the theoretical, abstractive tropes of absence and loss into specific narratives of environmental diasaster and extinction. What would an early poem look like, read anew, through the lens of eco-poetics? Here are lines from Merwin's early blank-verse poem, "Sea Monster," from *The Drunk in the Furnace*, a poem wholly allegory but refocused here in the light of environmental apocalypse:

[It] looked at us
For a long time, as though it knew us, but
Did not harm us . . . sinking at last,
The waters closing like a rush of breath. Then
We were all ashamed at what we had seen,
Said it was only a sea-trick or
A dream we had all had together. As it
May have been, for since then we have forgotten
How it was that, on sea or land, once
We proved to ourselves that we were awake.

What is the definition of prophecy? The subject we didn't know was there was there all along, waiting to emerge when we are ready to see it—even though, he says, we may be ashamed of what we find. Prophecy is foresight, seeing into the future; it is prediction, a saying-ahead-of. Perhaps not even Merwin has known the full range and possible subjects of his deepest gestures.

In fact, I think his work has moved in reverse order of traditional myth-making, in a final *via negativa*: evolving from the largest, most impersonal of myth-making—his first four books—toward an erasure of that myth and installation of a replacement myth, its negative, a mythos of nothingness; and, now, into the surprising focused, particular narrative of natural peril and extinction. Prophecy: only in aftersight can we tell its foresight. Here are lines from "The Sapphire," rhymed couplets from *Green with Beasts*, from exactly sixty years ago:

I stood on nothing in darkness,
Neither finding nor falling, without hope nor dread,
Not knowing pleasure nor discontented.
In time, like the first beam arriving from
The first star, a ray from a seed of light came. . . .
I recognized its visionary presence
By its clarity, its changeless patience,
And the unuttered joy that it was,
As the world's love before the world was.

Past the End Point: The Lice

Meghan O'Rourke

A lyric poem makes time into a physical thing: It parses our passing line by line. The best American poems do so, I would argue, by disrupting the linear rather than by reinforcing it: They complicate our transactional grasp of interval, replace our inner Google calendar with a daybook annotated by appointments with memory, inexplicable word-pictures, a future lit only by a dead star's light. They show us how the sun rose, "a ribbon at a time" (Dickinson) and imagine what it might be like to be found "underfoot" after we are gone (Whitman). A great lyric poem is a trapdoor to spiritual and ontological depths. It refracts our experience of time, making itself a totem and talisman, a "dumb old medallion" (Archibald MacLeish) that speaks to us, urgently.

W. S. Merwin's *The Lice* (1967), his sixth volume of poems, and to this day perhaps his most influential, is a book of crisis—ecological and political crisis, of a sort that feels all too familiar. A slim volume of dark, bleak lyrics that invoke various apocalypses—a denuded planet, the fruitless ravages of the Vietnam war, species extinction, a future of companionless isolation in which the dead are always proximate to us—*The Lice* signals that in addition to being a poet of myth and meditation Merwin would turn out to be one of our great American political poets. This might sound strange, because, with the exception of the famous poem "The Asians Are Dying," *The Lice* is almost entirely bereft of the historical and cultural references that we associate with political poetry.

In what way, you might ask, are the elusive poems in W. S. Merwin's *The Lice* political poems, and how does the "open form" he famously came to in this book speak to his developing political and ecological sensibility? In *The Lice*, Merwin tries to answer an unanswerable question, one that still matters to us today: How does a poet *voice* ecological devastation? How does a speaker envision an ecology beyond the human without reinforcing a kind of ethnocentric vision, or being inherently of the anthropocene era? How do you condemn war in a poem that is also open, flexible, and demands rereading? The answer, Merwin finds in *The Lice,* is to conjure a quasi-posthumous speaker who can't quite anchor him/herself in history or time, a predicament he embodies in a new use of line that is as disorienting as his former use of line was orienting or organizing. In "The Child," the speaker tells us:

> I pass skins withering in gardens that I see now
> Are not familiar
> And I have lost even the thread I thought I had.

Too often we associate political poetry with didacticism and an absence of art—think of Yeats's "out of the quarrel with others we make rhetoric; out of the quarrel with ourselves we make poetry"—and Merwin himself wrote of the danger of a political poem becoming a mere "loudspeaker." What I want to argue here is that rather than its politics being some kind of impediment to the aesthetic discoveries of *The Lice*, they were essential to it: its intricate art is fueled by what *The Paris Review* called a "savage ecological and political rage," and without the pressure of that rage, Merwin might never have found his new prosody. *The Lice*'s aesthetic exploration is forged in the crucible of feeling voiceless.

The weight of Merwin's increasing anger about politics and ecology—in the 1960s he took part in the nuclear disarmament movement, and began exploring environmentalism—created a new kind of formal pressure in the poems, generatively leading him to move beyond received myth toward making cosmologies from new, unused materials. He began writing these poems after the Cuban Missile Crisis and the publication of Rachel Carson's *Silent Spring* in 1962, when Americans were beginning to grapple with environmental issues and as the shadow of nuclear war still hung over them; during this period he moved back to America from England and then on to France, and while in France began trying to live off a kitchen garden. Uncoincidentally, the planet on view in *The Lice* is ruined, a place of "remembered metropoli" populated by the not-quite-dead, where people are alone except for nameless animals, in a land where they have "no voice" and death is evoked in terms of stellar and cosmic, not just mortal, extinction. Take "The Anniversary of My Death":

> Every year without knowing it I have passed the day
> When the last fires will wave to me
> And the silence will set out
> Tireless traveller
> Like the beam from a lightless star

The apocalyptic strain and loosening of form was already there in Merwin's previous book, *The Moving Target*. But it is in *The Lice* that Merwin completes the break with his former style—discarding the highly-wrought, organized, polished, Audenesque poems of the 1940s and 1950s. These poems eschew punctuation, so that the lines seem to hang in uncertain, vibrating relation to one another, without directing us how to read them. As he put it, "Punctuation nails the poem down on the page. When you don't use it the poem becomes more a thing in itself, at once more transparent and more actual." The poems in *The Lice* are nearly all voiced by a first person speaker and yet at times they seem almost not human. Helen Vendler has called this new poem as a "punctuationless short poem lacking (after its first line) initial capitals, a poem spoken to nobody within hearing distance, spoken to the air."

Crucially, this shift in Merwin's line changes the poem's relationship to time: no longer is it tidy, and ordered; now it is cosmic, enacted, alienating. As Merwin wrote in his seminal essay "On Open Form," published a year after the appearance of *The Lice*:

> What is called its form may be simply that part of the poem that had directly to do with time; the time of the poem, the time in which it was written, and the sense of recurrence in

> which the unique moment of vision is set. . . .
>
> In an age when time and technique encroach hourly. . . . on the source itself of poetry, it seems as though what is needed for any . . . poem is not a manipulable, more or less predictably recurring pattern, but an unduplicatable resonance, something that would be like an echo except that it is repeating no sound.

The absence of punctuation in *The Lice* allows the lines to resonate as he uses enjambment to disorient. The line break signals unpredictability and a failure of continuity (as well as a desperate need for it). It enacts the disruption of meaning, the speaker's sense that meaning is not a granary in which we store ourselves and transmit knowledge, but something encountered when we experience the destabilization of knowledge. "This is a world without syntax, inhabited by a man who thought he had read the signs correctly," Denis Donoghue noted in a 1967 review for *The New York Review of Books*, "and now, revising his texts, concludes that he was wrong." In "The Child," which I quoted from above, Merwin writes:

> I try to remember my faults to make sure
> one after the other but it is never
> satisfactory the list is never complete
>
> Then there are the stories and after a while I think something
> else must connect them besides just this me
> I regard myself starting the search turning
> Corners in remembered metropoli

The world is broken, and the speaker has "lost the thread": "I do not believe in knowledge as we know it," he tells us.

The opening poem, "The Animals," written mostly in couplets with two singleton lines, begins by evoking a speaker who has spent "all these years behind windows / with blind crosses sweeping the tables / and myself tracking over empty ground / Animals I never saw." At first we read the line, "myself tracking over empty ground," almost as a kind of self-referential statement, a description of searching for the self. But no: the search here is for animals, albeit ones that remain unseen, unrealized. The poem continues: "I with no voice / Remembering names to invent for them." This speaker has been deprived of voice, perhaps because he is socially powerless, an individual among the many, or rendered mute by the wrongs he sees around him, or, indeed, posthumous, wishfully hoping for change.

Merwin's use of negation—the "not and "never"—is also crucial to this new "open form" (an effect he may have learned from Wallace Stevens, one of his influences). Why negation? For one thing, negation humbly—yet powerfully—evokes the real: when you see the jacket of the newly dead hanging in a closet, you realize his absence viscerally. It also allows for a dialectic: as I say, "his shoes are gone," I conjure his shoes even as I acknowledge their absence. In Christian theology, one of the ways one can come to know God is by the *via negativa*, or apophetic theology, in which one defines God by what God is not. Here, Merwin reminds us of our temporariness, of the "real real," by defining perception around what we may not know, making this duality—I apprehend, I begin to understand, I fail to understand—a dynamic one on the level of syntax.

You can hear this technique in "The Widow," a poem that successfully articulates the book's vision of desolation. "There is no season that requires us," Merwin begins:

> You confide in images in things
> That can be represented which is their dimension you
> Require them you say This
> Is real and you do not fall down and moan
>
> Not seeing the irony in the air
>
> Everything that does not need you is real

Here, Merwin powerfully condemns the human belief that we

understand something about the world, all while failing to see what has escaped us and therefore is carried with us without our knowing. The book's title comes from a passage in Heraclitus, used as an epigraph to the book, that invokes lice as something we bring with us without ever realizing it.

Because of the way the lines hang here without the signposts of punctuation, time gets confused, doubles back and forward on itself, becomes a tesseract. The last poem in the book, "Looking for Mushrooms at Sunrise," seems explicitly to invoke Whitman's famous poem of unification, "Song of Myself," playing on and with Whitman's projection into a future he himself can't witness. Merwin begins by describing the speaker "walking on centuries of dead chestnut leaves / In a place without grief" in the time between night and dawn, when an oriole "Out of another life warns me / That I am awake." In the night, "The gold chanterelles pushed through a sleep that was not mine." Seeing them, the speaker realizes:

> Where they appear it seems I have been before
> I recognize their haunts as though remembering
> Another life
> Where else am I walking even now
> Looking for me

The speaker here, as in many of the poems, is cosmically suspended, aware of deep past and deep future. In this way, the speakers in *The Lice* often verge on a kind of posthumousness—each is fully human but has lost himself in a way that is crucial to his credibility as a moral guide. It is as if the poems seek to translate themselves into the utterances of something transhuman. Merwin wrote one of the most moving brief elegies in the English language, titled, simply, "Elegy": "Who would I show it to."

Now, for political poems these may seem curiously disconnected from historical reference points—more mystical than political. And yet they challenge our bedrock ideas of identity, pushing into almost transhistorical depths. In this way *The Lice* is a precursor for much that would come, a model for a moment when many poets likewise feel a civic discontent and that they speak "with no voice." It shows us, too, that we should have a more capacious idea of what political poetry really is: these poems are essentially meditative, probing traumas as one might probe a tooth coming loose, but they are indubitably eco-political, *dramatizing* human culpability. In *The Lice,* dogged by a sense of the world falling apart around him, Merwin found a style that not only allowed him to express his rage but to actually embody, in time, the disorientation produced by his apocalyptic sense of being at the end of something larger than ourselves. He found a voice for extinction that, paradoxically, carries past the end point of its possibility, like the light of dead star.

A Dazzling Darkness: William Merwin's Night

Rosanna Warren

A good poem takes its shape from its quest for knowledge, and its finished form on the page traces the form of its knowing. In his book *The Shadow of Sirius*, from 2008, William Merwin pursues knowledge with unusual determination and explicitness. Forms of the verb "to know" appear in almost every poem. And more often as verb than as the noun "knowledge," since the revelations Merwin seeks emerge as awareness of processes and ventures rather than as the static, contained product the noun suggests.

A quest to know what? For more than half a century, Merwin has been revolving the age-old question of our mortal being in time. It's the fundamental concern of poetry and song, language moving in time to commemorate our passing and our desire to remain: "Like as the waves make for the pebbled shore / So do our minutes hasten to their end. . . ." (Shakespeare, Sonnet 60). But Merwin has brought a particular, ecological consciousnessness to this meditation. As early as 1967, in *The Lice*, long before widespread public awareness of environmental disaster, Merwin murmured, "The extinct animals are still looking for their home" (in the poem ""In Autumn"), and the poem "The Last One" in that book staged a dark parable of a people destroying their land and in turn being destroyed by the shadow they have created: "Well they'd made up their minds to be everywhere because why not."

The conventional lyric preoccupation with time passing, then, translates for Merwin into the particular grief of time running out for many species of plants and animals, and perhaps for the earth itself. *The Shadow of Sirius* links that grief to the awareness of time running out for the aging poet himself, an awareness that doesn't provoke grief, but rather highlights experience and memory and paces acceptance. A real poem has real work to do. Merwin's work in *The Shadow of Sirius* is to metabolize the facts of loss and extinction--personal and general—into patterned psychic experience, beyond grief and panic, into a state, not passive, but wisely alert, with room for mourning and celebration in equal measure. The poems of this highly unified book achieve such transformation through style. With a rarefied diction (the words "silence," "darkness," and "hush" sound the bass-note throughout); with a fluid free verse steeped in remembered iambic cadences; with liturgical repetition; with the occasional lofting to the majesty of an ode ("o breath of morning," "The Nomad Flute,"), the *Sirius* poems usher the reader into a mysterious knowing beyond rational knowledge, and into an intuition about a language beyond words: "in its archaic / untaught language / that brings the bees to the rosemary" ("Heartland").

In its stylization and its celebration of song and the natural world, *The Shadow of Sirius* renews the genre of pastoral, darkened by elegy as it is in Theocritus and Virgil, in poems at once archaic and painfully contemporary. I would like to track their transformative work in two poems, "A Codex" and "The Nomad Flute":

You that sang to me once sing to me now
let me hear your long lifted note
survive with me
the star is fading
I can think farther than that but I forget
do you hear me

do you still hear me
does your air
remember you
o breath of morning
night song morning song
I have with me
all that I do not know
I have lost none of it

but I know better now

than to ask you
where you learned that music
where any of it came from
once there were lions in China

I will listen until the flute stops
and the light is old again

The poem immediately establishes intimacy between the speaker, "I," and the "you" who seems to be the flute remembered from long ago. In its simplicity and repetitiveness, all monosyllables, the first line sets the key for the book, and coordinates past and present: sang/sing; once/now. And though the poem is in free verse, this line has five stresses and ten syllables: it remembers the canonical English pentameter even while straying from it, in a book that is all about the sacramental efficacy of memory. It's worth asking why Merwin has divided the poem into irregular stanzas: other poems in the book are undivided, and still others are in subtly rhymed or unrhymed couplets. Here, the divisions mark stages in awareness. The first stanza issues commands: sing to me, let me hear, survive. The urgency of these imperatives rises from the threat of time passing and darkness encroaching: "the star is fading," and gives way to an equally urgent question: "do you hear me."

The second stanza repeats the question, increasing the anxiety with a temporal adverb: "do you *still* hear me." By now, in a magical reciprocity, the relationship of speaker to hearer has reversed: it's no longer a question of "I" hearing the flute, but of the flute hearing "me," and thereby granting "me" a larger measure of reality. The flute introduces a book that will be permeated by animism, a world in which light, tombstones, a glass, stones, and animals all share consciousness. Stanza two also introduces the theme of knowledge: "I have with me / all that I do not know / I have lost none of it." Which presents one of the book's fundamental strategies: paradox. In order to press beyond categories of rational knowledge, these poems all find ways of thrusting the reader into logical impasses from which one could emerge only in an intuitive, perhaps mystical leap. Here, we have the contradiction of an assertion of selfhood and possession ("I have with me") and a confession of ignorance, *lack* of possession ("all that I do not know"). The further claim, "I have lost none of it," is also self-contradictory, because what has not been lost is itself a condition of loss.

Stanza three carries us across the logical blockade with a new statement about knowledge in time: "but I know better now." This triumphal claim is immediately qualified, and elaborates a new understanding of knowledge as a kind of tact or wise ignorance: "but I know better now / than to ask you / where you learned that music." The one line that seems incongruous, because it makes a statement about positive rather than negative knowledge, is itself a statement of loss: "once there were lions in China." The final couplet in the future tense is the fruit of that new awareness: "I will listen until the flute stops / and the light is old again." A coordination of past and present and a stilling of appetite for information engender a future, though a precarious one—"until the flute stops." It is in the light of this vow, this listening, that the rest of the book will unfold. In yet another form of tact, the poet—usually the one speaking—here appears as a listener. And his delicately prefigured death appears not as a silencing of *his* voice, but as the silencing of the larger music he has been hearing.

"A Codex," by contrast, advances in couplets. It further differs from "The Nomad Flute" in pouring forward in one sentence and in enjambing emphatically. Merwin long ago abandoned punctuation, but his poems work themselves out in a wide variety of lineation and syntax, and "A Codex" staggers its quest for knowledge, its progress toward its last word "known," in a struggle between the arresting terraces of the couplets and the ongoing force of the sentence:

> It was a late book given up for lost
> again and again with its sentences
>
> bare at last and phrases that seemed transparent
> revealing what had been there the whole way

the poems of daylight after the day
lying open at last on the table

without explanation or emphasis
like sounds left when the syllables have gone

clarifying the whole grammar of waiting
not removing one question from the air

or closing the story although single lights
were beginning by then above and below

while the long twilight deepened its silence
from sapphire through opal to Athena's iris

until the shadow covered the gray pages
the comet words the book of presences

after which there was little to say
but then it was night and everything was known

Throughout *The Shadow of Sirius*, Merwin adjusts relations between time, knowledge, and language, and many of the poems point toward a language beyond words, an "archaic/untaught language / that brings the bees to the rosemary." "A Codex" is explicitly preoccupied by the problem of language conveying ineffable knowledge. And because human understanding and language occur in time, the poem structures its quest in a sequence of clauses marked by temporal adverbs: "*while* the long twilight," "*until* shadow," "*after* which," "but *then*."

The poem is a parable. The word "codex" means an ancient, bound manuscript, the early form of the book, and can refer specifically to a sacred text, such as Scripture, or to a body of laws and regulations. Merwin's poem moves teasingly between gestures of revelation ("sentences / bare at last," "phrase that seemed transparent/ revealing," "lying open at last on the table"), and gestures of occlusion ("a book given up for lost," "like sounds left when the syllables have gone"). This sacred book will not inform us in any conventional way. It will not remove "one question from the air" or close the story. What good is it, then? If we follow the poem's lead, we will "know better"—as in "The Nomad Flute"—than to ask such a question. We will submit to the pacing of the couplets as they restore a lost book but drain light from the pages, through twilight to shadow to night. We will entertain the possibility of a language persisting beyond semantics and even beyond phonetics. We will give up our demand for "presences" and for "comet words"—those brilliant, authoritative phrases. If the poem works, it works as a formal meditation to induct the reader into a state of quiet receptivity, an intimacy with emptiness and darkness in which ego dissolves and in which death may be imagined without panic. It resembles the conclusion of another poem in the book, "Far Along in the Story," where a boy listens to a flock of cranes until "the cranes were gone from the sky and at/ that moment he remembered who he was/ only he had forgotten his name."

Poems take their shapes from their quest for knowledge, I proposed. "A Codex" leads us on stepped couplets toward the paradox of an "everything" being known when it's night and nothing is known. Or when inadequate knowledge has fallen away. In "the Nomad Flute," "know" half-rhymes with "now," and opens into a knowledge maturing from the present into an imagined future. In the last line of "A Codex," "night" and "known" don't rhyme, but they alliterate. They precipitate a paradoxical counter-knowledge, "but then it was night and everything was known": a mystic chiaroscuro that echoes the paradox of the book's title, *The Shadow of Sirius*. Sirius, the dog-star, is the brightest star in our sky. What would be its shadow? It turns out that Sirius has a mysterious, smaller, partner-star, its shadow one might say, invisible for millennia, detected only in 1862. "A Codex" discovers this "deep but dazzling darkness" (to use Henry Vaughan's expression, in his poem "The Night"). In that darkness, we are invited to contemplate loss and extinction, not with hysteria and not with complacency, but with stoic clarity, and a kind of calm if not with peace.

The Nomad Flute

Stanley Plumly

You that sang to me once sing to me now

When I think of W. S. Merwin's immense body of work—some twenty-five volumes of lyric and extended poetry, plus many books of meditative prose, plus innumerable major translations of classic texts from major languages—when I think of Merwin's total body of writing, I am struck by how consistent the voice is in these different genres, especially in the poems, which is the source of where that voice is calling from. Anyone who has heard Merwin read his poetry aloud can hear that quiet richly authoritative quality of voice: I mean the listener can hear the Merwin music as Merwin himself seems to have heard it, written it down, then spoken it.

Such a quality of voice is, of course, not easy to define, since it lives inside its tone and timbre and visual texture, and even more difficult since it lives inside its implied content—the *how* of the voice inevitably tied to the *what* of the voice. One thing that is true of all good, not to say great writing is that its voice tends to be manifest: you can see it as well as hear it; it has an imaginative correspondence in much the same way that what we hear in music becomes visible in the mind's eye. Eliot, that great critical phrase-maker, tries to define the fact of this quality of voice as the "auditory imagination": "the feeling for syllable and rhythm, penetrating far below the conscious levels of thoughts and feeling, invigorating every word; sinking to the most primitive and forgotten, returning to the origin and bringing something back, seeking the beginning and the end."

If this is rather abstract and roundabout as a definition, perhaps it needs to be, since we are talking about the audible as ineffable. Eliot goes on to say that the auditory imagination "works through meanings, certainly, or not without meanings in the ordinary sense, and fuses the old and obliterated and the trite, the current, and the new and surprising, the most ancient and the most civilized mentality."

I find Eliot's use of the concept "mentality" to be cold, when what we are talking about is the warmest part of a poem—its voice, and the quality that makes that voice effective. I think Eliot's "mental" intention is to connect the grounded mind to the grounded heart in the celestial structures of the imagination, and to see in the dialectic between the old and the new, the familiar and the discovered the metaphor-making capacity of poetry, so that hearing a good poem in its right voice—either silently or literally—is to understand the word made flesh. What I find most compelling in the language of Eliot's formulation is his doting on words like "primitive" and "ancient," qualities almost Jungian in their suggestion of "returning to the origin and bringing something back . . . from far below the conscious levels of thoughts and feeling."

Merwin, more than any of our poets, speaks from that archetypal zone we associate with the primary, ancient, even classical imagination. It is as if he makes audible a dream language *a priori* to whatever the specific, particular, singular experience is. A poem like "Air," from *The Moving Target* (1963), is an obvious example of the Merwin speaker moving through an archetypal symbol-converted landscape at a time of day when such experience happens, as if whistling in the dark:

> Naturally it is night.
> Under the overturned lute with its
> One string I am going my way
> Which has a strange sound.
>
> This way the dust, that way the dust.
> I listen to both sides
> But I keep right on.

I remember the leaves sitting in judgment
And then winter.
I remember the rain with its bundle of roads.
The rain taking all its roads.
Nowhere.

Young as I am, old as I am.

I forget tomorrow, the blind man.
I forget the life among the buried windows.
The eyes in the curtains.
The wall
Growing through the immortelles.
I forget silence
The owner of the smile.

This must be what I wanted to be doing,
Walking at night between the two deserts,
Singing.

"Singing" is one of Merwin's stock answers as to how his voice functions in a poem—indeed, the word "song" comes up repeatedly throughout his work, either directly or by implication. But "song," for this poet, does not so much assume a strictly musical equivalency as it evokes a vocal arrangement of tone and emotion spoken out of hard-won wisdom—old, totemic, ancestral wisdom. One way to say it is that the ghost presence behind Merwin's best poems comes from the collective unconscious, for which he is an individual spokesperson, whose personal identity authenticates our shared individual and cultural narratives. Yet meta-song for Merwin is more than means and method, it is the substance, the lyric expression of language at a perfect level with meaning. In a poem by Merwin, what you see is what you hear—that calm, reconciling voice drawing horizon lines across the space and the volume of the experience.

In "Air," the speaker is moving between this way and that,

memory and its absence, under a sky of one lute string, in a world that feels reduced to just this moment, stripped of just about everything, yet a world that forces or gifts the speaker back into himself, into singing, into what the imagination is, which is something made out of what seems to be nothing, "night between the two deserts." "Air" is paced to be seen and heard within a greater purchase of white space and silence, a Beckett-like world of existential purity. As a poem it is an ars poetica, a baseline aesthetic statement.

Much has been made, and should be made, of Merwin's evolution as a formalist-cum-"free verse" poet. Compare the soft-hued off-and-on decasyllabic metrics of "Low Fields and Light" (1956) to the slanting rhyming couplets of "Grandfather in the Old Men's Home" (1960), to the relatively open patient form of "Air" (1963), with its conventional punctuation, to the completely open form of the love poem "When You Go Away" (1967), to the haiku-like chastity of "Man with One Leaf in October Night" (1970), to the experimental elegy for his father, "Strawberries" (1983), with its visually and vocally interrupted linear syntax, to the surface elegance of a poem like "Passing" (1996), to "The Nomad Flute" (2008), with its wistful invocation to the Muse, to the modulated ethereal evening first person voice of "Long Afternoon Light" (2014): compare this form-exploring career of subtle yet profound development and change within the traditional limits of what the lyric poem can be, and you still find the character of the Merwin voice to be a unified, consistent instrument—yes, a voice of natural variation but also, always, a lyrically civil understated voice that stays within itself, within its range, while, across time, it calls from the aural distances of our animistic past.

Compare, across a span of sixty years, the similar tone of voice, the landscape textures, the imaginative situation of "Low Fields and Light" with the new poem "Long Afternoon Light." We know from our decades of reading him that Merwin is essentially a sunset poet. He is also a poet, like Wordsworth, alone on the landscape, in a setting at once mythic yet self-contained. More than these identities, however—and more than the transformation of form from linear convention to a kind of flow-syntax in which the tensions are controlled by internal enjambments; and more than the deep silences within his language—is Merwin's brilliant rescue back to loneliness, back to spiritual isolation and natural connection, back to his ability to elevate the resonant feeling in his poems to a romance with the old gods. It would seem no accident that fresh out of Princeton Merwin would seek out the great English writer Robert Graves, on the Isle of Mallorca, and end up editing a good portion of Graves's classic *White Goddess*, the best book ever written on poetic myth, particularly on the archetype of the moon, in all its phases. Merwin's subsequent travels throughout the ancient Mediterranean and Provencal worlds stand at the beginning of his wandering, his nomadic search, his Continental education, and his commitment to an "international" style.

In "Low Fields and Light," the whole developing evening scene, in the speaker's mind's eye, is "Like a gray blade set to the moon's roundness, / Like a plain of glass touching all there is." This is an intimate pastoral vision enabled by its thoughtful, meditating distance ("I think it is Virginia. . . .") and understood in terms of that vision's disappearing moment, almost as if the poem were a landscape elegy for what the receiving eye is taking in. The example of disappearance in "Long Afternoon Light" is Merwin's response to those remembered lost small roads "written in sleep in the foothills / how long ago," in a mix of memory and the "moment of what is ours," a moment that "flows away out of reach." The theme, in both poems, separated by more than half-a-century, is fundamentally the same: the ephemeral nature of time as manifest in ephemeral nature.

And the tone of the voice is not only similar but dominant, since Merwin's art, like Stevens's art, is the art of tone: in Merwin's case it is a tone of wonderment, of acceptance, of a tacit reconciliation with the powers, be they small, great, or simply beautiful. But reconciliation, for Merwin, is not a giving-in; rather, it represents the implicit resistance to mortality that important art always provides. Much of that resistance has to do with Merwin's special genius through the function of his speakers, which is demonstrated best by their skill at standing outside themselves as observers while performing inside the poems as participants, as protagonists, so that the feeling of deep longing to hold onto what is past and passing never gets in the way of the immediacy of the imagination, which is why Merwin's first-person speakers invariably sound—and I emphasize the "sound" quality—like grammatical third-persons.

Because of the outside/inside double perspective in the point of view in so many of Merwin's poems, perhaps the most subtle quality in his lyric voice is the way it comes over as a secret to be shared, a voice that needs to bring the reader to the center of the intimacy of the circumstances. It is hard not to move your lips when reading a Merwin poem, as it moves almost *sotto voce* within the voicelessness of the page, as if the speaker were speaking from his dream, very quietly, to your dream, yet controlling the exchange from the aesthetic distance of discovered form. It works because his poetry's temperament is first of all formal and graceful and never overtly autobiographical, even when he uses names.

Merwin's poems are symbol-figures, masks that conceal in order to reveal. It matters, therefore, *how* they represent what they say, from the mouth of the darkness of the cave looking directly out into the light. Merwin is nearly ninety now, so he has developed a good deal of dream wisdom backed up behind him, including his own and our secrets. The remarkable thing is that from the start, from 1952 and *The Mask of Janus*, the Merwin voice has sounded well beyond its years, in a tone at once vulnerable yet majestical, haunted yet utterly confident, contemporaneous yet passed. I once asked Galway Kinnell, when we were teaching together at Princeton, if he and Merwin showed each other their poems when they were students there. He smiled, and said yes, but with the clarification that his poems were barehanded, even crude drafts compared to Merwin's finished, mature-like pieces. I would bet that Merwin's classic aural elegance was already in evidence.

The "aural imagination" is—if the idea of metaphor means anything anymore—a metaphor for enhancing how we see what we hear, the experience of which depends absolutely on the linguistic synesthesia only the imagination can provide. It can happen in a word or be created by the brickwork and ultimate structure of a poem, in the syntax and rhythm, yes, but in the silences too, in the silently aural give and take. I like especially the notion of it happening within the weight of a single word, the way Eliot's metaphoric patient is "etherized upon a table"—the brilliant sound of the verb "etherized" echoing its sense of paralysis.

In *The Lice*, one of Merwin's best books, published in 1967, there is a love poem that he left out of his *Selected,* doubtless for all kinds of personal reasons, one of which is that it was originally dedicated to his second wife, Dido. The poem has been restored in the Library of America edition of his work. "When You Go Away" is, I think, one of his most beautiful poems, and beautiful in the way it builds, through apparent discontinuity, its imagination, and beautiful in the way it sustains its manifest unity through tone:

> When you go away the wind clicks around to the north
> The painters work all day but at sundown the paint falls
> Showing the black walls
> The clock goes back to striking the same hour
> That has no place in the years
>
> And at night wrapped in the bed of ashes
> In one breath I wake
> It is the time when the beards of the dead get their growth
> I remember that I am falling
> That I am the reason
> And that my words are the garment of what I shall never be
> Like the tucked sleeve of a one-armed boy

I will not attempt the onerous task of trying to translate the images, except to say that they do add up (the domestic world suggested in the first stanza goes completely dark, isolated); and they do (in the first stanza) foreshadow the speaker's death associations with sleeplessness in the second stanza. We have moved, in the short course of the poem, from the rooms of the house in general to the bedroom, where, in his epiphany, the speaker suddenly understands that he is "the reason" for "when you go away." He also understands that this insight is an absolute—that "what I shall never be" is defined by the way the tucked sleeve stands for what is missing.

The poem moves with the concentration of a sonnet, whose lyric turn starts with the recognition line, "I remember that I am falling," and continues with the realization "That I am the reason" and concludes with the self-reflection on the poem itself "that my words are the garment of what I shall never be / Like the tucked sleeve of a one-armed boy." The "And" at the beginning of this ending "couplet" is rhetorically necessary because it picks up a certain soft drum-roll in the overall rhythm and pacing of the poem. The thought-rhyme of be/boy is crucial as well, as it speaks to the 15-year age difference between the younger Merwin and Dido, who once upon a time had been Graves's mistress. If I had to choose a powerful example of an auditory image, the closing of this poem would be it, with the emphasis on the word "tucked. That word seems to me to do all that is required of its onomatopoetic opportunity. In Merwin's one-armed boy image it is the adjective "tucked" that seems to me to do the onomatopoetic job of the seeing in the hearing required. The sleeve is tucked, not pinned nor tied nor rolled up tight. It is tucked, as if temporary, as if promising something that can never happen. And it is a boy's arm, not a man's; it is against the natural order of things. The tucked image magnifies what is lost when you go away, while the garment, like a remnant of the sleeve will never, in the longest line of the poem, be unfurled. "Tucked" has a temporary, exposed aspect, something of the moment, something naked. The fact that it is a boy's arm magnifies what is lost when you go away, while the garment of the sleeve will never be what it is meant to be, even if unfurled in the longest line of the poem.

In a poem from only a few years ago, Merwin writes that "I have with me/all that I do not know/I have lost none of it." Whatever, ontologically, he still does not know, he knows the feeling of what that feels like. Merwin, above all our poets, is the poet of Longing, of the human condition Eliot once described as being able to imagine a fulfillment we can never have. The music of Merwin's imagination is, word for modulated word, the heard equivalent of the correlatives he conjures to represent this truth. You read a Merwin poem here and there in a magazine, you read through the latest collection of those poems as gathered in a particular year, you read two or three books of his poetry in sequence, then you think about the whole sweep of the poetry, the twenty and more major volumes, plus the year after year publication of non-fiction prose and translations, and you come away aware that Merwin's life's work is a monument not just to talent but to courage, you come away knowing this is what a whole life is.

About the Authors

David Baker is author or editor of many books, most recently *Scavenger Loop* (poems, W. W. Norton, 2015) and *Show Me Your Environment: Essays on Poetry, Poets, and Poems* (University of Michigan Press, 2014). His collection, *Never-Ending Birds*, was awarded the Theodore Roethke Memorial Poetry Prize in 2011. Baker writes widely about lyric poetry, American literature, and poetic form. He holds the Thomas B. Fordham Chair at Denison University and serves as Poetry Editor of *The Kenyon Review*.

Linda Gregerson is author of six collections of poetry, most recently *Prodigal: New and Selected Poems* (Houghton Mifflin Harcourt 2015). She has received awards from the American Academy of Arts and Letters, Modern Poetry Association, Institute for Advanced Study, National Humanities Center, Rockefeller Foundation, and is a member of the American Academy of Arts and Sciences and a Chancellor of the Academy of American Poets. She is Distinguished University Professor at the University of Michigan.

Meghan O'Rourke is the author of the best-selling memoir, *The Long Goodbye* (Riverhead, 2011) and three books of poetry, most recently *Sun in Days* (W. W. Norton, 2017). The recipient of a Guggenheim Fellowship, a Whiting Award, and a Radcliffe Fellowship for her nonfiction, she teaches at NYU and Princeton. She is at work on a book about mysterious illnesses and the intersection of culture and medicine.

Carl Phillips's most recent book of poetry is *Reconnaissance* (FSG, 2015), winner of the PEN/USA Award in Poetry and the Lambda Literary Award for Gay Poetry. A new collection, *Wild Is the Wind*, will be released in 2018. Phillips has also written two books of prose, most recently *The Art of Daring: Risk, Restlessness, Imagination* (Graywolf, 2014), and he has translated Sophocles's *Philoctetes* (Oxford, 2004). He teaches at Washington University in Saint Louis.